How to Write and Speak
Correct English

Published by :
Lotus Press Publishers & Distributors

How to Write and Speak Correct English

Reena Gupta

4735/22, Prakash Deep Building
Ansari Road, Darya Ganj,
New Delhi - 110002

Lotus Press : Publishers & Distributors
Unit No. 220, 2nd Floor, 4735/22, Prakash Deep Building,
Ansari Road, Darya Ganj, New Delhi- 110002
Ph.: 41325510, 98118-38000
• E-mail : lotuspress1984@gmail.com
www.lotuspress.co.in

How to Write and Speak Correct English

ISBN: 978-81-8382-231-2

Printed & Published by : **Lotus Press Publisher & Distributors,** New Delhi-02

Preface

English is an international language and is one of the most popular and most spoken in the world. English is very much important in our daily life—it is necessary in each and every field. If we know English we never feel tongue tide in front of others. It is a widely spoken language. People take pride in speaking English If we don't know English, we will leg behind the others. We need to know English language in order to study any science subject or any computer language. We need to know English to communicate effectively too many developed countries.

Unfortunately, there is no easy route to write or speak better English. The way you use English has more to do with the environment you grew up in, the books you have been exposed to, the people you associate with, and the level of your education. If you want to write or speak better English, the best way to go about it is to read good books and make some friends who speak in the way you want to.

This comprehensive and easy-to-follow book will help to express yourself in speaking and writing English, clearly, correctly and persuasively. It is designed to demolish the writer's block and liberate the tongue-tied speaker. It will help you to choose your words carefully, arrange them with precision and communicate your message effectively. This book is ideal for students in middle school through college, homeschoolers, and all who wanted to improve their skills in English.

-Author

Contents

1

Importance of English Language

English is a West Germanic language which is the dominant language in the United Kingdom, the United States, many Commonwealth nations including Australia, Canada, New Zealand and other former British colonies. It is the most spoken language in the world. It is estimated that there are 380 million native speakers and 300 million who use English as a second language and a further 100 million use it as a foreign language. It is the language of science, aviation, computing, diplomacy, and tourism. It is listed as the official or co-official language of over 45 countries and is spoken extensively in other countries where it has no official status. English plays a part in the cultural, political or economic life of many countries.

Origin of English

English is an Anglo-Frisian language brought to Britain in the 5th Century AD by Germanic settlers from various parts of northwest Germany. The original Old English language was subsequently influenced by two successive waves of invasion. The first was by speakers of languages in the Scandinavian branch of the Germanic family, who colonised parts of Britain in the 8th and 9th centuries. The second wave was of the Normans in the 11th century, who spoke Norman.

The history of the language can be traced back to the arrival of three Germanic tribes to the British Isles during the 5th Century AD. Angles, Saxons and Jutes crossed the North Sea from what is the present day Denmark and northern Germany. The inhabitants of Britain previously spoke a Celtic language. This was quickly displaced. Most of the Celtic speakers were pushed into Wales, Cornwall and Scotland. One group migrated to the Brittany Coast of France where their descendants still speak the Celtic Language of Breton today. The Angles were named from Engle, their land of origin. Their language was called Englisc from which the word, English derives. It is convenient to divide English into periods—Old English (or Anglo-Saxon; to c.1150), Middle English (to c.1500), and Modern English.

Old English

The invaders dominated the original Celtic-speaking inhabitants, whose languages survived largely in Scotland, Wales, and Cornwall. The dialects spoken by the invaders formed what is now called Old English. Later, it was strongly influenced by the North Germanic language Norse, spoken by the Vikings who settled mainly in the north-east. The new and the earlier settlers spoke languages from different branches of the Germanic family; many of their lexical roots were the same or similar, although their grammars were more distant, including the prefixes, suffixes and inflections of many of their words. The Germanic language of these Old English inhabitants of Britain was influenced by the contact with Norse invaders, which may have been responsible for some of the morphological simplification of Old English, including loss of grammatical gender and explicitly marked case (with the notable exception of the pronouns). The most famous work from the Old English period is the epic poem "Beowulf", by an unknown poet.

The introduction of Christianity added the first wave of Latin and Greek words to the language. It has been argued that the Danish contribution continued into the early Middle Ages.

The Old English period ended with the Norman conquest, when the language was influenced, to an even greater extent, by the Norman French-speaking Normans. The use of Anglo-Saxon to describe a merging of Anglian and Saxon languages and cultures is a relatively modern development. According to Lois Fundis, "The first citation for the second definition of 'Anglo-Saxon', referring to early English language or a certain dialect thereof, comes during the reign of Elizabeth I, from a historian named Camden, who seems to be the person most responsible for the term becoming well-known in modern times."

Middle English

For the 300 years following the Norman Conquest in 1066, the Norman kings and the high nobility spoke only a variety of French called Anglo-Norman. English continued to be the language of the common people. While the Anglo-Saxon Chronicle continued until AD 1154, most other literature from this period was in Old French or Latin. A large number of Norman words were assimilated into Old English, with some words doubling for Old English words (for instance, ox/beef, sheep/mutton). The Norman influence reinforced the continual evolution of the language over the following centuries, resulting in what is now referred to as Middle English. Among the changes was a broadening in the use of a unique aspect of English grammar, the "continuous" tenses, with the suffix "-ing".

English spelling was also influenced by French in this period, with the /è/ and /ð/ sounds being spelled rather than with the letters þ and ð, which did not exist in

French. During the 15th century, Middle English was transformed by the Great Vowel Shift, the spread of a standardised London-based dialect in government and administration, and the standardising effect of printing. Modern English can be traced back to around the time of William Shakespeare. The most well-known work from the Middle English period is Geoffrey Chaucer's The Canterbury Tales.

Various contemporary sources suggest that within fifty years most of the Normans outside the royal court had switched to English, with French remaining the prestige language largely out of social inertia. For example, Orderic Vitalis, a historian born in 1075 and the son of a Norman knight, said that he only learned French as a second language.

English literature starts to reappear circa AD 1200, when a changing political climate, and the decline in Anglo-Norman, made it more respectable. By the end of that century, even the royal court had switched back to English. Anglo-Norman remained in use in specialised circles for a while longer, but it had ceased to be a living language.

Modern English

From the late 15th century, the language changed into Modern English, often dated from the Great Vowel Shift.

English is continuously assimilating foreign words, especially Latin and Greek, causing English to have the largest vocabulary of any language in the world. As there are many words from different languages the risk of mispronunciation is high, but remnants of the older forms remain in a few regional dialects, notably in the West Country. In 1755 Samuel Johnson published the first significant English dictionary.

American English and other Varieties

Also significant beginning around 1600 AD was the English colonisation of North America and the subsequent creation of American English. Some pronunciations and usages "froze" when they reached the American shore. In certain respects, some varieties of American English are closer to the English of Shakespeare than modern Standard English ('English English' or as it is often incorrectly termed 'British English') is. Some "Americanisms" are actually originally English English expressions that were preserved in the colonies while lost at home (e.g., fall as a synonym for autumn, trash for rubbish, and loan as a verb instead of lend).

The American dialect also served as the route of introduction for many native American words into the English language. Most often, these were place names like Mississippi, Roanoke, and Iowa. Indian-sounding names like Idaho were sometimes created that had no native-American roots. But, names for other things besides places were also common. Raccoon, tomato, canoe, barbecue, savanna, and hickory have native American roots, although in many cases the original Indian words were mangled almost beyond recognition.

Spanish has also been great influence on American English. Mustang, canyon, ranch, stampede, and vigilante are all examples of Spanish words that made their way into English through the settlement of the American West. A lesser number of words have entered American English from French and West African languages.

Likewise dialects of English have developed in many of the former colonies of the British Empire. There are distinct forms of the English language spoken in Australia, New Zealand, South Africa, India and many other parts of the world.

Spread of English

English is currently one of the most widely spoken and written languages worldwide, with some 380 million native speakers.

Through the global influence of native English speakers in cinema, music, broadcasting, science, and the Internet in recent decades, English is now the most widely learned second language in the world.

Because a working knowledge of English is required in many fields and occupations, education ministries around the world mandate the teaching of English to at least a basic level.

And there are some other facts about English you might be interested in knowing. In no particular order, here are some of the numbers about English:

- English is the most widespread language in the world and is more widely spoken and written than any other language.
- Over 400 million people use the English vocabulary as a mother tongue, only surpassed in numbers, but not in distribution by speakers of the many varieties of Chinese.
- Over 700 million people, speak English, as a foreign language.
- Did you know that of all the world's languages English is arguably the richest in vocabulary; and that the *Oxford English Dictionary* lists about 500,000 words, and there are a half-million technical and scientific terms still uncatalogued?
- Three-quarters of the world's mail, telexes and cables are in English.
- More than half of the world's technical and scientific periodicals are in English.

- English is the medium for 80 per cent of the information stored in the world's computers.
- English is the language of navigation, aviation and of Christianity; it is the ecumenical language of the World Council of Churches.
- Five of the largest broadcasting companies in the world (CBS, NBC, ABC, BBC and CBC) transmit in English, reaching millions and millions of people all over the world.

The main language used throughout the world on the internet is English. The media that make up the Internet are overwhelmingly American in origin, so it is no wonder that the mother tongue of the Web is English. Four factors determine the degree to which a given language finds use on the Internet:

1. The number of users of the language
2. The extent of its use as an official language
3. The economic power of the language, and
4. The volume of information disseminated in that language.

Today, English reigns supreme in all four respects. It is studied as a foreign language throughout the world and employed by a majority of Internet users. Of the 163 member nations of the U.N., more use English as their official language than any other. The easiest way to calculate the economic influence of a language may be to add up the gross domestic products (GDP) of all the nations where it is spoken. People who count English as their mother tongue make up less than 10 per cent of the world's population, but possess over 30 per cent of the world's economic power. Therefore, in terms of the quantity of transmitted information, English is the leader by far. After English, 26 nations in the U.N. cite French as their official tongue, 21 Spanish and 17 Arabic. Each of

Table 1. English Speaking Countries. Majority English speaking populations are shown in bold.

Antigua	Kenya (with Swahili)	Sierra Leone
Australia	Kiribati	Singapore (with Malay, Mandarin and Tamil)
Bahamas	Lesotho (with Sotho)	**South Africa** (with Afrikaans, Xhosa and Zulu)
Barbados	Liberia	Surinam (with Dutch)
Belize	Malawi (with Chewa)	Swaziland (with Swazi)
Bermuda	Malta (with Maltese)	Tanzania (with Swahili)
Botswana	Mauritius	Tonga (with Tongan)
Brunei (with Malay)	Namibia (with Afrikaans)	**Trinidad and Tobago**
Cameroon (with French)	Nauru (with Nauruan)	Tuvalu
Canada (with French)	**New Zealand**	Uganda
Dominica	Nigeria	**United Kingdom** and its dependences
Fiji	Pakistan (with Urdu)	**United States of America** and its dependencies
Gambia	Papua New Guinea	Vanatu (with French)
Ghana	Philippines (with Tagalog)	Western Samoa (with Samoan)
Grenada	Puerto Rico (with Spanish)	Zambia
Guyana	**St Christopher and Nevis**	Zimbabwe
India (with several Indian languages)	**St Lucia**	
Ireland (with Irish Gaelic)	**St Vincent**	
Jamaica	Senegal (with French)	
	Seychelles (with French)	

these three languages forms a sizable linguistic constituency on the Internet.

Importance of English

A language is a systematic means of communication by the use of sounds or conventional symbols. It is the code we all use to express ourselves and communicate to others. It is a communication by word of mouth. It is the mental faculty or power of vocal communication. It is a system for communicating ideas and feelings using sounds, gestures, signs or marks. Any means of communicating ideas, specifically, human speech, the expression of ideas by the voice and sounds articulated by the organs of the throat and mouth is a language. This is a system for communication. A language is the written and spoken methods of combining words to create meaning used by a particular group of people.

Language, so far as we know, is something specific to humans, that is to say it is the basic capacity that distinguishes humans from all other living beings. Language therefore remains potentially a communicative medium capable of expressing ideas and concepts as well as moods, feelings and attitudes.

A set of linguists who based their assumptions of language on psychology made claims that language is nothing but 'habit formation'. According to them, language is learnt through use, through practice. In their view, 'the more one is exposed to the use of language, the better one learns'.

Written languages use symbols to build words. The entire set of words is the language's vocabulary. The ways in which the words can be meaningfully combined is defined by the language's syntax and grammar. The actual meaning of words and combinations of words is defined by the language's semantics.

The latest and the most advanced discoveries and inventions in science and technology are being made in the universities located in the United States of America where English language is the means of scientific discourse.

English is the prominent international language in communications, science, business, aviation, entertainment, and diplomacy and also on the Internet, and the language most often studied as a foreign language in the European Union, followed by French, German, and Spanish. It is also the most studied in the People's Republic of China, India, Japan, South Korea, and Taiwan.

A degree in English can lead to many different careers. While it is a first step to becoming an English language and literature teacher in secondary schools, those who study English also go on to become, among other things, translators, editors, journalists, public relations managers, or administrators in the arts, the humanities and in NGOs. The linguistic as well as the critical and analytical skills developed in the study of literature are an important asset for those interested in fields such as international law and international business.

English is one of the most important languages in the world. It can even be said to be the single most important language. Yes, other languages are important too, but not for the same reasons as English is important. English is important because it is, maybe, the only language that truly links the whole world together. If not for English, the whole world may not be as united as it is today. The other languages may be important for their local values and culture.

English can be used as a language in any part of the world. This is because at least a few people in each locality would know the language. Though these people might not have the same accent as others, the language at least will be understandable. There are various reasons for the importance of English language. They are listed below.

1. *Travel*: When a person travels to another part of the world either for the sake of business or even as a tourist, the languages may differ. In these conditions, English is the language that helps people to deal with the situation. It is like a universal language.
2. *Same country*: In countries like India, where the land is so vast with people of various cultures live, the languages of each part of the country also differ. Under the circumstances, English can be the only link as people in each place will not be able to learn all the other languages to communicate with the people. English bridges this gap and connects the people.
3. *Education/studies*: The presence of English as a universal language assumes importance in the fact that more and more people leave their countries not only for the sake of business and pleasure, but also for studying. Education has increased the role of English. People who go to another country to study can only have English as their medium of study. This is because the individual will not be able to learn a subject in the local language of the country. This again reinforces the fact that English language is very important.
4. *Correspondence*: All correspondences between offices in different countries and also between political leaders of various countries is in English. This linking factor also tells of the importance of English language.

5. *Business*: With 80 per cent of international business communications written in English and most of the world's trade and financial business transacted in the language, companies worldwide acknowledge the necessity of having an English speaking workforce. In today's competitive world, everyone needs skills that will equip them for a changing work environment. Technical and communication skills are highly desired by companies yet proficiency in English is essential for many posts.
5. *Internet*: In spite of the growth of Internet in various languages, English is the mainstay of the Internet users. This is the language in which most of the information and websites are available. It is very difficult to translate each and every relevant webpage into the language of various countries. With Internet becoming very important in E commerce and also in education, English language is bound to grow. Thus the importance of English as a language is emphasised.

The historical circumstances of India (having been ruled by the British for over two centuries) have given the Indians an easy access to mastering English language, and innumerable opportunities for advancement in the field of science and technology. Many Indians have become so skilled in English language and have won many international awards for creative and comparative literatures during the last few years. Sometime ago, an Indian author, Arundhati Roy, won the prestigious booker prize for her book *The God of Small Things*. Her book sold lakhs of copies all over the globe.

Over the years, English language has become one of our principal assets in getting a global leadership for books written by Indian authors and for films made by Indians in English language. A famous Indian moviemaker Shekhar Kapoor's film "Elizabeth" has got several nominations for Oscar Awards. It does not require any further argument to establish the advantage English language has brought to us at the international level.

English language comes to our aid in our commercial transactions throughout the globe. English is the language of the latest business management in the world and Indian proficiency in English has brought laurels to many Indian business managers. English is a means not only for international commerce; it has become increasingly essential for inter-state commerce and communication.

In India, people going from North to South for education or business mostly communicate in English, which has become a link language. Keeping this in mind, the Parliament has also recognised English as an official language in addition to Hindi. All the facts of history and developments in present day India underline the continued importance of learning English in addition to vernaculars.

Some of the states of India are witnessing popular increase in public demand for teaching of English language from the primary classes. Realising the importance, recently, the Minister of Indian Railways, Laloo Prasad Yadav, demands teaching of English language in schools. The great demand for admission in English medium schools throughout the country is a testimony to the attraction of English to the people of India. Many of the leaders, who denounce English, send their own children to English medium schools. Many of the schools in the country have English as the sole or additional medium of instruction.

A language attracts people because of the wealth of literature and knowledge enshrined in it. English poses no danger to Indian languages. The Indian languages are vibrant and are developing by the contributions of great minds using them as their vehicle of expression. English is available to us as a historical heritage in addition to our own language. We must make the best use of English to develop ourselves culturally and materially so that we can compete with the best in the world of mind and matter. English language is our window to the world.

English language is one tool to establish our viewpoint. We can learn from others experience. We can check the theories of foreigners against our experience. We can reject the untenable and accept the tenable. We can also propagate our theories among the international audience and readers.

We can make use of English to promote our worldview and spiritual heritage throughout the world. Swami Vivekananda established the greatness of Indian view of religion at the world conference of religions in Chicago in 1893. He addressed the gathering in impressive English. Many spiritual gurus have since converted thousands of English people to our spirituality by expressing their thought and ideas in masterful English. English has thus become an effective means of promoting Indian view of life, and strengthening our cultural identity in the world.

When William Caxton setup his printing press in London (1477) the new hybrid language (vernacular English mixed with courtly French and scholarly Latin) became increasingly standardised, and by 1611, when the Authorised (King James) Version of the *Bible* was published, the educated English of London had become the core of what is now called Standard English. By the time of Johnson's dictionary (1755) and the American Declaration of Independence (1776), English was international and recognisable as the language we use today. The Orthography of English was more or less established by 1650 and, in England in particular, a form of standard educated speech, known as Received Pronunciation (RP) spread from the major public schools in the 19th century. This accent was adopted in the early 20th century by the British Broadcasting Corporation (BBC) for its announcers and readers, and is variously known as RP, BBC English, Oxford English, and the King's or Queen's English.

Generally, Standard English today does not depend on accent but rather on shared educational experience, mainly of the printed language. Present-day English is an immensely varied language, having absorbed material from many other tongues. It is spoken by more than 300 million native speakers, and between 400 and 800 million foreign users. It is the official language of air transport and shipping; the leading language of science, technology, computers, and commerce; and a major medium of education, publishing, and international negotiation. For this reason, scholars frequently refer to its latest phase as World English.

The future of English as a language is very secure. In this era of consolidation and trying to unify various aspects of life, it will not be long before English can be made as a single language of the world like the single currency and the union of various nations.

2

Understanding English Grammar

English grammar is a group of structural rules which describe how words combine with each other to form sentences. So, the important thing to remember is that grammar is really necessary to communicate more effectively. English is universal, but around the world we can find many forms of English, for example, between American and British dialects there are many points of grammar where they differ.

English grammar tends to fall into two groups: The Descriptivist—describe the patterns through which meanings are typically created in functional speech and writing, and the Prescriptivist—set out pre-existing rules as to how meanings are created?

This chapter describes the basic rules of English grammar that would be helpful for you to write and speak English correctly.

The three essentials of the English language are: Purity, Perspicuity and Precision.

Purity precludes the use of all slang words, vulgar phrases, obsolete terms, foreign idioms, ambiguous expressions or any ungrammatical language whatsoever. Neither does it sanction the use of any newly coined word until such word is adopted by the best writers and speakers.

Perspicuity demands the clearest expression of thought conveyed in unequivocal language, so that there may be no misunderstanding whatever of the thought or idea the speaker or writer wishes to convey. All ambiguous words, words of double meaning and words that might possibly be construed in a sense different from that intended, are strictly forbidden. Perspicuity requires a style at once clear and comprehensive and entirely free from pomp and pedantry and affectation or any straining after effect.

Precision requires concise and exact expression, free from redundancy and tautology, a style terse and clear and simple enough to enable the hearer or reader to comprehend immediately the meaning of the speaker or writer. It forbids, on the one hand, all long and involved sentences, and, on the other, those that are too short and abrupt. Its object is to strike the golden mean in such a way as to rivet the attention of the hearer or reader on the words uttered or written.

Divisions of Grammar

In order to speak and write the English language correctly, it is imperative that the fundamental principles of the Grammar be mastered, for no matter how much we may read of the best authors, no matter how much we may associate with and imitate the best speakers, if we do not know the underlying principles of the correct formation of sentences and the relation of words to one another, we will be to a great extent like the parrot, that merely repeats what it hears without understanding the import of what is said. Of course the parrot, being a creature without reason, cannot comprehend; it can simply repeat what is said to it, and as it utters phrases and sentences of profanity with as much facility as those of virtue, so by like analogy, when we do not understand the grammar of the language, we may be making egregious blunders while thinking we are speaking with the utmost accuracy.

There are four great divisions of grammar, viz.: orthography, etymology, syntax, and prosody.

1. *Orthography* treats of letters and the mode of combining them into words.
2. *Etymology* treats of the various classes of words and the changes they undergo.
3. *Syntax* treats of the connection and arrangement of words in sentences.
4. *Prosody* treats of the manner of speaking and reading and the different kinds of verse.

The three first mentioned concern us most.

Letters

A letter is a mark or character used to represent an articulate sound. Letters are divided into vowels and consonants. A vowel is a letter which makes a distinct sound by itself. Consonants cannot be sounded without the aid of vowels. The vowels are a, e, i, o, u, and sometimes w and y when they do not begin a word or syllable.

Syllables and Words

A syllable is a distinct sound produced by a single effort of shall, pig, dog. In every syllable there must be at least one vowel. A word consists of one syllable or a combination of syllables. Many rules are given for the dividing of words into syllables, but the best is to follow as closely as possible the divisions made by the organs of speech in properly pronouncing them.

PARTS OF SPEECH

All the words in the English language are divided into nine great classes. These classes are called the Parts of Speech. They are Article, Noun, Adjective, Pronoun, Verb, Adverb, Preposition, Conjunction and Interjection. Of these, the Noun is the most important, as all the others are more or less dependent upon it.

A Noun signifies the name of any person, place or thing, in fact, anything of which we can have either thought or idea. There are two kinds of Nouns, Proper and Common. Common Nouns are names which belong in common to a race or class, as man, city. Proper Nouns distinguish individual members of a race or class as Ritu, Mumbai. In the former case man is a name which belongs in common to the whole race of mankind, and city is also a name which is common to all large centres of population, but Ritu signifies a particular individual of the race, while Mumbai denotes a particular one from among the cities of the world.

Nouns are varied by Person, Number, Gender, and Case. Person is that relation existing between the speaker, those addressed and the subject under consideration, whether by discourse or correspondence. The Persons are First, Second and Third and they represent respectively the speaker, the person addressed and the person or thing mentioned or under consideration.

Number is the distinction of one from more than one. There are two numbers, singular and plural; the singular denotes one, the plural two or more. The plural is generally formed from the singular by the addition of 's' or 'es'.

Gender has the same relation to nouns that sex has to individuals, but while there are only two sexes, there are four genders, viz., masculine, feminine, neuter and common. The masculine gender denotes all those of the male kind, the feminine gender all those of the female kind, the neuter gender denotes inanimate things or whatever is without life, and common gender is applied to animate beings, the sex of which for the time being is indeterminable, such as fish, mouse, bird, etc. Sometimes things which are without life as we conceive it and which, properly speaking, belong to the neuter gender, are, by a figure of speech called Personification, changed into either the masculine or feminine gender, as, for instance, we say of the sun, He is rising; of the moon, She is setting.

Case is the relation one noun bears to another or to a verb or to a preposition. There are three cases, the Nominative, the Possessive and the Objective. The nominative is the subject of which we are speaking or the agent which directs the action of the verb; the possessive case denotes possession, while the objective indicates the person or thing which is affected by the action of the verb.

An Article is a word placed before a noun to show whether the latter is used in a particular or general sense. There are but two articles, a or an and the.

An Adjective is a word which qualifies a noun, that is, which shows some distinguishing mark or characteristic belonging to the noun.

Article

An Article is a word placed before a noun to show whether the noun is used in a particular or general sense.

There are two articles, a or an and the. A or an is called the indefinite article because it does not point put any particular person or thing but indicates the noun in its widest sense; thus, a man means any man whatsoever of the species or race.

The is called the definite article because it points out some particular person or thing; thus, the man means some particular individual.

Noun

A noun is the name of any person, place or thing as Rohan, India, book. Nouns are proper and common.

- *Proper nouns* are names applied to particular persons or places.
- *Common nouns* are names applied to a whole kind or species.

Nouns are inflected by number, gender and case.

- *Number* is that inflection of the noun by which we indicate whether it represents one or more than one.
- *Gender* is that inflection by which we signify whether the noun is the name of a male, a female, of an inanimate object or something which has no distinction of sex.
- *Case* is that inflection of the noun which denotes the state of the person, place or thing represented, as the subject of an affirmation or question, the owner or possessor of something mentioned, or the object of an action or of a relation.

Thus in the example, "Karan tore the leaves of Kajol's book," the distinction between book which represents only one object and leaves which represent two or more objects of the same kind is called Number; the distinction of sex between Karan, a male, and Kajol, a female, and book and leaves, things which are inanimate and neither male nor female, is called Gender; and the distinction of state between the person who tore the book, and the subject of the affirmation, Kajol, the owner of the book, leaves the objects torn, and book the object related to leaves, as the whole of which they were a part, is called Case.

Adjective

An adjective is a word which qualifies a noun, that is, shows or points out some distinguishing mark or feature of the noun; as, *A black dog.*

Adjectives have three forms called degrees of comparison, the positive, the comparative and the superlative.

- *The positive* is the simple form of the adjective without expressing increase or diminution of the original quality: nice.
- *The comparative* is that form of the adjective which expresses increase or diminutión of the quality: nicer.
- *The superlative* is that form which expresses the greatest increase or diminution of the quality: nicest. or

An adjective is in the positive form when it does not express comparison; as, "A rich man."

An adjective is in the comparative form when it expresses comparison between two or between one and a number taken collectively, as, "Karan is richer than Mohan"; "he is richer than all the men in Mumbai."

An adjective is in the superlative form when it expresses a comparison between one and a number of individuals taken separately; as, "Karan is the richest man in Mumbai."

Adjectives expressive of properties or circumstances which cannot be increased have only the positive form; as, A circular road; the chief end; an extreme measure.

Adjectives are compared in two ways, either by adding er to the positive to form the comparative and *est* to the positive to form the superlative, or by prefixing more to the positive for the comparative and most to the positive for the superlative; as, handsome, handsomer, handsomest or handsome, more handsome, most handsome.

Adjectives of two or more syllables are generally compared by prefixing more and most.

Many adjectives are irregular in comparison; as, Bad, worse, worst; Good, better, best.

Pronoun

A pronoun is a word used in place of a noun; as, "Rohan gave his pen to Rajesh and he lent it to Ritu to write her copy with it." Without the pronouns we would have to write this sentence,—"Karan gave Karan's pen to Mohan and Mohan lent the pen to Rani to write Rani's copy with the pen."

There are three kinds of pronouns—Personal, relative and adjective pronouns.

— *Personal pronouns* are so called because they are used instead of the names of persons, places and things. The Personal Pronouns are I, Thou, He, She, and It, with their plurals, We, Ye or You and They. I is the pronoun of the first person because it represents the person speaking.

  Thou is the pronoun of the second person because it represents the person spoken to.

  He, She, It are the pronouns of the third person because they represent the persons or things of whom we are speaking. Like nouns, the Personal Pronouns have number, gender and case. The gender of the first and second person is obvious, as they represent the person or persons speaking and those who are addressed. The personal pronouns are thus declined:

First Person
Male or Female

	Singular	*Plural*
N.	I	We
P.	Mine	Ours
O.	Me	Us

Second Person
Male or Female

	Singular	*Plural*
N.	Thou	You
P.	Thine	Yours
O.	Thee	You

Third Person
Male

	Singular	*Plural*
N.	He	They
P.	His	Theirs
O.	Him	Them

Third Person
Female

	Singular	*Plural*
N.	She	They
P.	Hers	Theirs
O.	Her	Them

Third Person
Neuter

	Singular	*Plural*
N.	It	They
P.	Its	Theirs
O.	It	Them

In colloquial language and ordinary writing Thou, Thine and Thee are seldom used, except by the Society of Friends. The Plural form You is used for both the nominative and objective singular in the second person and Yours is generally used in the possessive in place of Thine. The Relative Pronouns are so called because they relate to some word or phrase going before; as, "The boy who told the truth;" "He has done well, which gives me great pleasure."

Here who and which are not only used in place of other words, but who refers immediately to boy, and which to the circumstance of his having done well.

The word or clause to which a relative pronoun refers is called the Antecedent.

– *Relative pronouns* are who, which, that and what.

Who is applied to persons only; as, "The man who was here."

Which is applied to the lower animals and things without life; as, "The horse which I sold." "The hat which I bought."

That is applied to both persons and things; as, "The friend that helps." "The bird that sings." "The knife that cuts."

What is a compound relative, including both the antecedent and the relative and is equivalent to that which; as, "I did what he desired," i.e. "I did that which he desired."

Relative pronouns have the singular and plural alike.

Who is either masculine or feminine; which and that are masculine, feminine or neuter; what as a relative pronoun is always neuter.

That and what are not inflected.

Who and which are thus declined.

Who, which and what when used to ask questions are called Interrogative Pronouns.

— *Adjective pronouns* partake of the nature of adjectives and pronouns and are subdivided as follows:

  — *Demonstrative adjective pronouns* which directly point out the person or object. They are this, that with their plurals these, those, and yon, same and selfsame.

  — *Distributive adjective pronouns* used distributively. They are each, every, either, neither.

  — *Indefinite adjective pronouns* used more or less indefinitely. They are any, all, few, some, several, one, other, another, none.

  — *Possessive adjective pronouns* denoting possession. They are my, thy, his, her, its, our, your, their. The possessive adjective pronouns differ from the possessive case of the personal pronouns in that the latter can stand alone while the former cannot. "Who owns that book?" "It is mine." You cannot say "it is my,"—the word book must be repeated.

The Verb

A verb is a word which implies action or the doing of something, or it may be defined as a word which affirms, commands or asks a question. Thus, the words John the table, contain no assertion, but when the word strikes is introduced, something is affirmed, hence the word strikes is a verb and gives completeness and meaning to the group. The simple form of the verb without inflection is called the root of the verb; e.g. love is the root of the verb,—"To Love."

Verbs are regular or irregular, transitive or intransitive. A verb is said to be regular when it forms the past tense by adding 'ed' to the present or 'd' if the verb ends in e. When its past tense does not end in ed it is said to be irregular.

A transitive verb is one the action of which passes over to or affects some object; as "I struck the table." Here the action of striking affected the object table, hence struck is a transitive verb. An intransitive verb is one in which the action remains with the subject; as "I walk," "I sit," "I run." Many intransitive verbs, however, can be used transitively; thus, "I walk the horse;" walk is here transitive.

Verbs are inflected by number, person, tense and mood. Number and person as applied to the verb really belong to the subject; they are used with the verb to denote whether the assertion is made regarding one or more than one and whether it is made in reference to the person speaking, the person spoken to or the person or thing spoken about.

Tense

In their tenses verbs follow the divisions of time. They have present tense, past tense and future tense with their variations to express the exact time of action as to an event happening, having happened or yet to happen.

Moods

There are four simple moods—the Infinitive, the Indicative, the Imperative and the Subjunctive.

The Mood of a verb denotes the mode or manner in which it is used. Thus if it is used in its widest sense without reference to person or number, time or place, it is in the Infinitive Mood; as "To run." Here we are not told who does the running, when it is done, where it is done or anything about it.

When a verb is used to indicate or declare or ask a simple question or make any direct statement, it is in the Indicative Mood. "The boy loves his book." Here a direct statement is made concerning the boy. "Have you a pin?" Here a simple question is asked which calls for an answer. When the verb is used to express a command or entreaty it is in the Imperative Mood as, "Go away." "Give me a penny."

When the verb is used to express doubt, supposition or uncertainty or when some future action depends upon a contingency, it is in the subjunctive mood; as, "If I come, he shall remain."

Many grammarians include a fifth mood called the potential to express power, possibility, liberty, necessity, will or duty. It is formed by means of the auxiliaries may, can, ought and must, but in all cases it can be resolved into the indicative or subjunctive. Thus, in "I may write if I choose," "may write" is by some classified as in the potential mood, but in reality the phrase I may write is an indicative one while the second clause, if I choose, is the expression of a condition upon which, not my liberty to write, depends, but my actual writing.

Verbs have two participles, the present or imperfect, sometimes called the active ending in ing and the past or perfect, often called the passive, ending in 'ed' or 'd'.

The infinitive expresses the sense of the verb in a substantive form, the participles in an adjective form; as "To rise early is healthful." "An early rising man." "The newly risen sun."

The participle in ing is frequently used as a substantive and consequently is equivalent to an infinitive; thus, "To rise early is healthful" and "Rising early is healthful" are the same. The principal parts of a verb are the Present Indicative, Past Indicative and Past Participle; as:

Love	Loved	Loved

Sometimes one or more of these parts are wanting, and then the verb is said to be defective.

Can	Could
May	Might
Shall	Should
Will	Would
Ought	Ought

Verbs may also be divided into principal and auxiliary. A principal verb is that without which a sentence or clause can contain no assertion or affirmation. An auxiliary is a verb joined to the root or participles of a principal verb to express time and manner with greater precision than can be done by the tenses and moods in their simple form. Thus, the sentence, "I am writing an exercise; when I shall have finished it I shall read it to the class." has no meaning without the principal verbs writing, finished read; but the meaning is rendered more definite, especially with regard to time, by the auxiliary verbs am, have, shall. There are nine auxiliary or helping verbs, viz., Be, have, do, shall, will, may, can, ought, and must. They are called helping verbs, because it is by their aid the compound tenses are formed.

To Be

The verb To Be is the most important of the auxiliary verbs. It has eleven parts, viz., am, art, is, are, was, wast, were, wert; be, being and been.

Voice

The active voice is that form of the verb which shows the Subject not being acted upon but acting; as, "The cat catches mice." "Charity covers a multitude of sins."

The passive voice: When the action signified by a transitive verb is thrown back upon the agent, that is to say, when the subject of the verb denotes the recipient of the action, the verb is said to be in the passive voice. "Karan was loved by his neighbours." Here Karan the subject is also the object affected by the loving, the action of the verb is thrown back on him, hence the compound verb was loved is said to be in the passive voice. The passive voice is formed by putting the perfect participle of any transitive verb with any of the eleven parts of the verb To Be.

Conjugation

The conjugation of a verb is its orderly arrangement in voices, moods, tenses, persons and numbers.

Here is the complete conjugation of the verb "Love"—Active Voice.

Principle Parts

Present	*Past*	*Past Participle*
Love	Loved	Loved

Infinitive Mood

To Love

Indicative Mood

Present Tense

	Sing.	*Plural*
1st person	I love	We love
2nd person	You love	You love
3rd person	He loves	They love

Past Tense

	Sing.	*Plural*
1st person	I loved	We loved
2nd person	You loved	You loved
3rd person	He loved	They loved

Future Tense

	Sing.	*Plural*
1st person	I shall love	They will love
2nd person	You will love	You will love
3rd person	He will love	We shall love

Present Perfect Tense

	Sing.	*Plural*
1st person	I have loved	We have loved
2nd person	You have loved	You have loved
3rd person	He has loved	They have loved

Past Perfect Tense

	Sing.	*Plural*
1st person	I had loved	We had loved
2nd person	You had loved	You had loved
3rd person	He had loved	They had loved

Future Perfect Tense

	Sing.	*Plural*
1st person	I shall have loved	We shall have loved
2nd person	You will have loved	You will have loved
3rd person	He will have loved	They will have loved

Imperative Mood

(Present tense only)

	Sing.	*Plural*
2nd person	Love (you)	Love (you)

Subjunctive Mood

Present Tense

	Sing.	*Plural*
1st person	If I love	If we love
2nd person	If you love	If you love
3rd person	If he love	If they love

Past Tense

	Sing.	*Plural*
1st person	If I loved	If we loved
2nd person	If you loved	If you loved
3rd person	If he loved	If they loved

Present Perfect Tense

	Sing.	*Plural*
1st person	If I have loved	If we have loved
2nd person	If you have loved	If you have loved
3rd person	If he has loved	If they have loved

Past Perfect Tense

	Sing.	*Plural*
1st person	If I had loved	If we had loved
2nd person	If you had loved	If you had loved
3rd person	If he had loved	If they had loved

Infinitives

Present	Perfect
To love	To have loved

Participles

Present	Past Perfect
Loving Loved	Having loved

Conjugation of "To Love"

Passive Voice

Indicative Mood

Present Tense

	Sing.	*Plural*
1st person	I am loved	We are loved
2nd person	You are loved	You are loved
3rd person	He is loved	They are loved

Past Tense

	Sing.	*Plural*
1st person	I was loved	We were loved
2nd person	You were loved	You were loved
3rd person	He was loved	They were loved

Future Tense

	Sing.	*Plural*
1st person	I shall be loved	We shall be loved
2nd person	You will be loved	You will be loved
3rd person	He will be loved	They will be loved

Present Perfect Tense

	Sing.	*Plural*
1st person	I have been loved	We have been loved
2nd person	You have been loved	You have been loved
3rd person	He has been loved	They have been loved

Past Perfect Tense

	Sing.	*Plural*
1st person	I had been loved	We had been loved
2nd person	You had been loved	You had been loved
3rd person	He had been loved	They had been loved

Future Perfect Tense

	Sing.	*Plural*
1st person	I shall have been loved	We shall have been loved
2nd person	You will have been loved	You will have been loved
3rd person	He will have been loved	They will have been loved

Imperative Mood

(Present Tense Only)

	Sing.	*Plural*
2nd person	Be (you) loved	Be (you) loved

Subjunctive Mood

Present Tense

	Sing.	*Plural*
1st person	If I be loved	If we be loved
2nd person	If you be loved	If you be loved
3rd person	If he be loved	If they be loved

Past Tense

	Sing.	*Plural*
1st person	If I were loved	If they were loved
2nd person	If you were loved	If you were loved
3rd person	If he were loved	If we were loved

Present Perfect Tense

	Sing.	*Plural*
1st person	If I have been loved	If we have been loved
2nd person	If you have been loved	If you have been loved
3rd person	If he has been loved	If they have been loved

Past Perfect Tense

	Sing.	*Plural*
1st person	If I had been loved	If we had been loved
2nd person	If you had been loved	If you had been loved
3rd person	If he had been loved	If they had been loved

Infinitives

Present	Perfect
To be loved	To have been loved

Participles

Present	Past	Perfect
Being loved	Been loved	Having been loved

Note that the plural form of the personal pronoun, you, is used in the second person singular throughout. The old form thou, except in the conjugation of the verb "To Be," may be said to be obsolete. In the third person singular he is representative of the three personal pronouns of the third person, He, She and It.

Adverb

An adverb is a word which modifies a verb, an adjective or another adverb. Thus, in the example—"He writes well," the adverb shows the manner in which the writing is performed; in the examples—"He is remarkably diligent" and "He works very faithfully," the adverbs modify the adjective diligent and the other adverb faithfully by expressing the degree of diligence and faithfulness.

Adverbs are chiefly used to express in one word what would otherwise require two or more words; thus, There signifies in that place; whence, from what place; usefully, in a useful manner. Adverbs, like adjectives, are sometimes varied in their terminations to express comparison and different degrees of quality.

Some adverbs form the comparative and superlative by adding er and est; as, soon, sooner, soonest. Adverbs which end in ly are compared by prefixing more and most; as, nobly, more nobly, most nobly. A few adverbs are irregular in the formation of the comparative and superlative; as, well, better, best.

Preposition

A preposition connects words, clauses, and sentences together and shows the relation between them. "My hand is on the table" shows relation between hand and table. Prepositions are so called because they are generally placed before the words whose connection or relation with other words they point out.

Conjunction

A conjunction joins words, clauses and sentences; as "Ram and Shyam". "My father and mother have come, but I have not seen them." The conjunctions in most general use are and, also; either, or; neither, nor; though, yet; but, however; for, that; because, since; therefore, wherefore, then; if, unless, lest.

Interjection

An interjection is a word used to express some sudden emotion of the mind. Thus in the examples,—"Ah! there he comes; alas! what shall I do?" ah, expresses surprise, and alas, distress. Nouns, adjectives, verbs and adverbs become interjections when they are uttered as exclamations, as, nonsense! strange! hail! away! etc. We have now enumerated the parts of speech and as briefly as possible stated the functions of each. As they all belong to the same family they are related to one another but some are in closer affinity than others.

To point out the exact relationship and the dependency of one word on another is called parsing and in order that every etymological connection may be distinctly understood a brief resume of the foregoing essentials is here given:

The signification of the noun is limited to one, but to any one of the kind, by the indefinite article, and to some particular one, or some particular number, by the definite article.

Nouns, in one form, represent one of a kind, and in another, any number more than one; they are the names of males, or females, or of objects which are neither male nor female; and they represent the subject of an affirmation, a command or a question,—the owner or possessor of a thing,—or the object of an action, or of a relation expressed by a preposition.

Adjectives express the qualities which distinguish one person or thing from another; in one form they express quality without comparison; in another, they express comparison between two, or between one and a number taken collectively,—and in a third they express comparison between one and a number of others taken separately.

Pronouns are used in place of nouns; one class of them is used merely as the substitutes of names; the pronouns of another class have a peculiar reference to some preceding words in the sentence, of which they are the substitutes,—and those of a third class refer adjectively to the persons or things they represent. Some pronouns are used for both the name and the substitute; and several are frequently employed in asking questions.

Affirmations and commands are expressed by the verb; and different inflections of the verb express number, person, time and manner. With regard to time, an affirmation may be present or past or future; with regard to manner, an affirmation may be positive or conditional, it being doubtful whether the condition is fulfilled or not, or it being implied that it is not fulfilled—

the verb may express command or entreaty; or the sense of the verb may be expressed without affirming or commanding. The verb also expresses that an action or state is or was going on, by a form which is also used sometimes as a noun, and sometimes to qualify nouns.

Affirmations are modified by adverbs, some of which can be inflected to express different degrees of modification. Words are joined together by conjunctions; and the various relations which one thing bears to another are expressed by 'prepositions. Sudden emotions of the mind, and exclamations are expressed by interjections. Some words according to meaning belong sometimes to one part of speech, sometimes to another. Thus, in "After a storm comes a calm," calm is a noun; in "It is a calm evening," calm is an adjective; and in "Calm your fears," calm is a verb.

The following sentence containing all the parts of speech is parsed etymologically:

"I now see the old man coming, but, alas, he has walked with much difficulty."

- *I,* a personal pronoun, first person singular, masculine or feminine gender, nominative case, subject of the verb see.
- *now,* an adverb of time modifying the verb see.
- *see,* an irregular, transitive verb, indicative mood, present tense, first person singular to agree with its nominative or subject I.
- *the,* the definite article particularising the noun man.
- *old,* an adjective, positive degree, qualifying the noun man.
- *man,* a common noun, third person singular, masculine gender, objective case governed by the transitive verb see.

- *coming*, the present or imperfect participle of the verb "to come" referring to the noun man.
- *but*, a conjunction.
- *alas*, an interjection, expressing pity or sorrow.
- *he*, a personal pronoun, third person singular, masculine gender, nominative case, subject of verb has walked.
- *has walked*, a regular, intransitive verb, indicative mood, perfect tense, third person singular to agree with its nominative or subject he.
- *with*, a preposition, governing the noun difficulty.
- *much*, an adjective, positive degree, qualifying the noun difficulty.
- *difficulty*, a common noun, 3rd person singular, neuter gender, objective case governed by the preposition with.

The Sentence

A sentence is an assemblage of words so arranged as to convey a determinate sense or meaning, in other words, to express a complete thought or idea. No matter how short, it must contain one finite verb and a subject or agent to direct the action of the verb.

"Birds fly;" "Fish swim;" "Men walk;"—are sentences.

A sentence always contains two parts, something spoken about and something said about it. The word or words indicating what is spoken about form what is called the subject and the word or words indicating what is said about it form what is called the predicate.

In the sentences given, birds, fish and men are the subjects, while fly, swim and walk are the predicates.

Types of Sentences

There are three kinds of sentences, simple, compound and complex.

1. *The simple sentence* expresses a single thought and consists of one subject and one predicate, as, "Man is mortal."
2. *A compound sentence* consists of two or more simple sentences of equal importance the parts of which are either expressed or understood, as "The men work in the fields and the women work in the household," or "The men work in the fields and the women in the household" or "The men and women work in the fields and in the household."
3. *A complex sentence* consists of two or more simple sentences so combined that one depends on the other to complete its meaning; as; "When he returns, I shall go on my vacation." Here the words, "when he returns" are dependent on the rest of the sentence for their meaning.

   A clause is a separate part of a complex sentence, as "when he returns" in the last example.

   A phrase consists of two or more words without a finite verb.

   Without a finite verb we cannot affirm anything or convey an idea, therefore we can have no sentence.

Infinitives and participles which are the infinite parts of the verb cannot be predicates. "I looking up the street" is not a sentence, for it is not a complete action expressed. When we hear such an expression as "A dog running along the street," we wait for something more to be added, something more affirmed about the dog, whether he bit or barked or fell dead or was run over.

Thus in every sentence there must be a finite verb to limit the subject. When the verb is transitive, that is, when the action cannot happen without affecting something, the thing affected is called the object. Thus in "Bhima killed Kichaka" the action of the killing affected Kichaka. In "The cat has caught a mouse," mouse is the object of the catching.

Arrangement of Words in Sentence

Of course in simple sentences the natural order of arrangement is subject—verb—object. In many cases no other form is possible. Thus in the sentence "The cat has caught a mouse," we cannot reverse it and say "The mouse has caught a cat" without destroying the meaning, and in any other form of arrangement, such as "A mouse, the cat has caught," we feel that while it is intelligible, it is a poor way of expressing the fact and one which jars upon us more or less.

In longer sentences, however, when there are more words than what are barely necessary for subject, verb and object, we have greater freedom of arrangement and can so place the words as to give the best effect. The proper placing of words depends upon perspicuity and precision. These two combined give style to the structure.

Most people are familiar with Gray's line in the immortal Elegy—"The ploughman homeward plods his weary way." This line can be paraphrased to read 18 different ways. Here are a few variations:

> Homeward the ploughman plods his weary way.
> The ploughman plods his weary way homeward.
> Plods homeward the ploughman his weary way.
> His weary way the ploughman homeward plods.
> Homeward his weary way plods the ploughman.
> Plods the ploughman his weary way homeward.
> His weary way the ploughman plods homeward.
> His weary way homeward the ploughman plods.
> The ploughman plods homeward his weary way.
> The ploughman his weary way plods homeward.

and so on. It is doubtful if any of the other forms are superior to the one used by the poet. Of course his arrangement was made to comply with the rhythm and rhyme of the verse. Most of the variations depend upon the emphasis we wish to place upon the different words.

In arranging the words in an ordinary sentence we should not lose sight of the fact that the beginning and end are the important places for catching the attention of the reader. Words in these places have greater emphasis than elsewhere.

In Gray's line the general meaning conveyed is that a weary ploughman is plodding his way homeward, but according to the arrangement a very slight difference is effected in the idea. Some of the variations make us think more of the ploughman, others more of the plodding, and still others more of the weariness.

As the beginning and end of a sentence are the most important places, it naturally follows that small or insignificant words should be kept from these positions. Of the two places the end one is the more important, therefore, it really calls for the most important word in the sentence. Never commence a sentence with And, But, Since, Because, and other similar weak words and never end it with prepositions, small, weak adverbs or pronouns.

The parts of a sentence which are most closely connected with one another in meaning should be closely connected in order also. By ignoring this principle many sentences are made, if not nonsensical, really ridiculous and ludicrous. For instance: "Ten thousand rupees reward is offered for information of any person injuring this property by order of the owner." "This monument was erected to the memory of Shyam, who was shot by his affectionate brother."

In the construction of all sentences the grammatical rules must be inviolably observed. The laws of concord, that is, the agreement of certain words, must be obeyed.

1. The verb agrees with its subject in person and number. "I have," "Thou hast," (the pronoun thou is here used to illustrate the verb form, though it is almost obsolete), "He has", show the variation of the verb to agree with the subject. A singular subject calls for a singular verb, a plural subject demands a verb in the plural; as," "The boy writes", "The boys write".

   The agreement of a verb and its subject is often destroyed by confusing *(a)* collective and common nouns; *(b)* foreign and English nouns; *(c)* compound and simple subjects; *(d)* real and apparent subjects.

   A collective noun is a number of individuals or things regarded as a whole; as, class regiment. When the individuals or things are prominently brought forward, use a plural verb; as The class were distinguished for ability. When the idea of the whole as a unit is under consideration employ a singular verb; as The regiment was in camp.

   It is sometimes hard for the ordinary individual to distinguish the plural from the singular in foreign nouns, therefore, he should be careful in the selection of the verb. He should look up the word and be guided accordingly. "He was an alumnus of Harvard." "They were alumni of Harvard."

   When a sentence with one verb has two or more subjects denoting different things, connected by and, the verb should be plural; as, "Snow and rain are disagreeable." When the subjects denote the same thing and are connected by or the verb should be singular; as, "The man or the woman is to blame."

When the same verb has more than one subject of different persons or numbers, it agrees with the most prominent in thought; as, "He, and not you, is wrong." "Whether he or I am to be blamed."

2. Never use the past participle for the past tense nor vice versa. This mistake is a very common one. At every turn we hear "He done it" for "He did it." "The jar was broke" instead of broken. "He would have went" for "He would have gone," etc.

3. The use of the verbs shall and will is a rock upon which even the best speakers come to wreck. They are interchanged recklessly.

   Their significance changes according as they are used with the first, second or third person. With the first person shall is used in direct statement to express a simple future action; as, "I shall go to the city tomorrow." With the second and third persons shall is used to express a determination; as, "You shall go to the city tomorrow," "He shall go to the city tomorrow."

   With the first person will is used in direct statement to express determination, as, "I will go to the city tomorrow." With the second and third persons will is used to express simple future action; as, "You will go to the city tomorrow," "He will go to the city tomorrow."

   A very old rule regarding the uses of shall and will is thus expressed in rhyme:

   > In the first person simply shall foretells,
   > In will a threat or else a promise dwells.
   > Shall in the second and third does threat,
   > Will simply then foretells the future feat.

4. Take special care to distinguish between the nominative and objective case. The pronouns are the only words which retain the ancient distinctive

case ending for the objective. Remember that the objective case follows transitive verbs and prepositions. Don't say "The boy who I sent to see you," but "The boy whom I sent to see you." Whom is here the object of the transitive verb sent. Don't say "She bowed to him and I" but "She bowed to him and me" since me is the objective case following the preposition to understood. "Between you and I" is a very common expression. It should be "Between you and me" since between is a preposition calling for the objective case.

5. Be careful in the use of the relative pronouns who, which and that. Who refers only to persons; which only to things; as, "The boy who was drowned," "The umbrella which I lost." The relative that may refer to both persons and things; as, "The man that I saw." "The hat that I bought."

6. Don't use the superlative degree of the adjective for the comparative; as "He is the richest of the two" for "He is the richer of the two." Other mistakes often made in this connection are:

   (a) Using the double comparative and superlative; as, "These apples are much more preferable." "The most universal motive to business is gain."

   (b) Comparing objects which belong to dissimilar classes; as "There is no nicer life than a teacher."

   (c) Including objects in class to which they do not belong; as, "The fairest of her daughters, Eve."

   (d) Excluding an object from a class to which it does belong; as, "Arjun was braver than any ancient warrior."

7. Don't use an adjective for an adverb, or an adverb for an adjective. Don't say, "He acted nice towards

me" but "He acted nicely toward me," and instead of saying "She looked beautifully" say "She looked beautiful."

8. Place the adverb as near as possible to the word it modifies. Instead of saying, "He walked to the door quickly," say "He walked quickly to the door."
9. Not alone be careful to distinguish between the nominative and objective cases of the pronouns, but try to avoid ambiguity in their use.

Classes of Sentences

There are two great classes of sentences according to the general principles upon which they are founded. These are termed the loose and the periodic.

In the loose sentence the main idea is put first, and then follow several facts in connection with it. Defoe is an author particularly noted for this kind of sentence. He starts out with a leading declaration to which he adds several attendant connections. For instance in the opening of the story of Robinson Crusoe we read: "I was born in the year 1632 in the city of York, of a good family, though not of that country, my father being a foreigner of Bremen, who settled first at Hull; he got a good estate by merchandise, and leaving off his trade lived afterward at York, from whence he had married my mother, whose relations were named Robinson, a very good family in the country and from I was called Robinson Kreutznaer; but by the usual corruption of words in England, we are now called, nay, we call ourselves, and write our name Crusoe, and so my companions always called me,"

In the periodic sentence the main idea comes last and is preceded by a series of relative introductions. This kind of sentence is often introduced by such words as that, if, since, because. The following is an example:

"That through his own folly and lack of circumspection he should have been reduced to such circumstances as to be forced to become a beggar on the streets, soliciting alms from those who had formerly been the recipients of his bounty, was a sore humiliation."

On account of its name many are liable to think the loose sentence an undesirable form in good composition but this should not be taken for granted. In many cases it is preferable to the periodic form. As a general rule in speaking, as opposed to writing, the loose form is to be preferred, inasmuch as when the periodic is employed in discourse the listeners are apt to forget the introductory clauses before the final issue is reached. Both kinds are freely used in composition, but in speaking, the loose which makes the direct statement at the beginning should predominate. As to the length of sentences much depends on the nature of the composition.

However the general rule may be laid down that short sentences are preferable to long ones. The tendency of the best writers of the present day is towards short, snappy, pithy sentences which rivet the attention of the reader. They adopt as their motto *multum in parvo* (much in little) and endeavour to pack a great deal in small space. Of course the extreme of brevity is to be avoided. Sentences can be too short, too jerky, too brittle to withstand the test of criticism. The long sentence has its place and a very important one. It is indispensable in argument and often is very necessary to description and also in introducing general principles which require elaboration.

In employing the long sentence the inexperienced writer should not strain after the heavy, ponderous type. Johnson and Carlyle used such a type, but remember, an ordinary mortal cannot wield the sledge hammer of a giant. Johnson and Carlyle were intellectual giants and few can hope to stand on the same literary pedestal. The tyro in composition should never seek after the heavy style. The best of all authors in the English language for style is Addison. Macaulay says: "If you wish a style learned, but not pedantic, elegant but not ostentatious, simple yet refined, you must give your days and nights to the volumes of Joseph Addison." The simplicity, apart from the beauty of Addison's writings causes us to reiterate the literary command—"Never use a big word when a little one will convey the same or a similar meaning."

Macaulay himself is an elegant stylist to imitate. He is like a clear brook kissed by the noon-day sun in the shining bed of which you can see and count the beautiful white pebbles. Goldsmith is another writer whose simplicity of style charms.

The beginner should study these writers, make their works his *vade mecum*, they have stood the test of time and there has been no improvement upon them yet, nor is there likely to be, for their writing is as perfect as it is possible to be in the English language. Apart from their grammatical construction there can be no fixed rules for the formation of sentences. The best plan is to follow the best authors and these masters of language will guide you safely along the way.

The Paragraph

The paragraph may be defined as a group of sentences that are closely related in thought and which serve one common purpose. Not only do they preserve the sequence of the different parts into which a composition is divided, but they give a certain spice to the matter like raisins in a plum pudding. A solid page of printed matter is distasteful to the reader; it taxes the eye and tends towards the weariness of monotony, but when it is broken up into sections it loses much of its heaviness and the consequent lightness gives it charm, as it were, to capture the reader. Paragraphs are like stepping-stones on the bed of a shallow river, which enable the foot passenger to skip with ease from one to the other until he gets across; but if the stones are placed too far apart in attempting to span the distance one is liable to miss the mark and fall in the water and flounder about until he is again able to get a foothold. 'This the same with written language, the reader by means of paragraphs can easily pass from one portion of connected thought to another and keep up his interest in the subject until he gets to the end.

Throughout the paragraph there must be some connection in regard to the matter under consideration,—a sentence dependency. For instance, in the same paragraph we must not speak of a house on fire and a runaway horse unless there is some connection between the two. We must not write consecutively:

"The fire raged with fierce intensity, consuming the greater part of the large building in a short time." "The horse took fright and wildly dashed down the street scattering pedestrians in all directions." These two sentences have no connection and therefore should occupy separate and distinct places. But when we say—"The fire raged with fierce intensity consuming the greater part of the large building in a short time and the horse taking fright at the flames dashed wildly down the street scattering pedestrians in all directions,"—there is a natural sequence, viz., the horse taking fright as a consequence of the flames and hence the two expressions are combined in one paragraph.

As in the case of words in sentences, the most important places in a paragraph are the beginning and the end. Accordingly the first sentence and the last should by virtue of their structure and nervous force, compel the reader's attention. It is usually advisable to make the first sentence short; the last sentence may be long or short, but in either case should be forcible. The object of the first sentence is to state a point clearly; the last sentence should enforce it.

It is a custom of good writers to make the conclusion of the paragraph a restatement or counterpart or application of the opening. In most cases a paragraph may be regarded as the elaboration of the principal sentence. The leading thought or idea can be taken as a nucleus and around it constructed the different parts of the paragraph.

Anyone can make a context for every simple sentence by asking himself questions in reference to the sentence. Thus—"The foreman gave the order"— suggests at once several questions; "What was the order?" "to whom did he give it?" "why did he give it?" "what was the result?" etc. These questions when answered will depend upon the leading one and be an elaboration of it into a complete paragraph.

If we examine any good paragraph we shall find it made up of a number of items, each of which helps to illustrate, confirm or enforce the general thought or purpose of the paragraph. Also the transition from each item to the next is easy, natural and obvious; the items seem to come of themselves. If, on the other hand, we detect in a paragraph one or more items which have no direct bearing, or if we are unable to proceed readily from item to item, especially if we are obliged to rearrange the items before we can perceive their full significance, then we are justified in pronouncing the paragraph construction faulty.

No specific rules can be given as to the construction of paragraphs. The best advice is,—Study closely the paragraph structure of the best writers, for it is only through imitation, conscious or unconscious of the best models, that one can master the art.

3

How to Write Correctly?

Experiences in school leave some people with the impression that good writing simply means writing that contains no bad mistakes—that is, no errors of grammar, punctuation, or spelling. In fact, good writing is much more than just correct writing. It's writing that responds to the interests and needs of our readers.

Here are the basic characteristics of good, effective writing:

- Good writing has a clearly defined purpose.
- It makes a clear point.
- It supports that point with specific information.
- The information is clearly connected and arranged.
- The words are appropriate, and the sentences are clear, concise, emphatic, and correct.

Good writing is the result of much practice and hard work. This fact should encourage you: it means that the ability to write well is not a gift that some people are born with, not a privilege extended to only a few. If you're willing to work, you can improve your writing.

Don't be discouraged by the thought that writing rarely comes easily to anyone. Instead, keep in mind that regular practice will make you a better writer. As you sharpen your skills, you will gain confidence and enjoy writing more than you did before.

Writing Process

Once we've made the decision to work to improve our writing, we need to think about exactly what we will be working on. In other words, we need to consider how we handle the various steps involved in the whole process of writing: from discovering ideas for a topic, through successive drafts, to a final revision and proofreading.

Let's look at how three students have described the steps that they typically follow when writing a paper:

- Before doing anything, I make sure I've got a quiet room and a clear head. When I feel ready to work, I sit in front of my laptop and begin tapping out whatever comes to mind. Then, after taking a short walk, I read over what I've written and pick out the things that strike me as worth keeping—key ideas and interesting details. After this, I usually go on to compose a rough draft pretty quickly. Then (maybe in a day or two, if I've gotten an early start) I read the draft and add explanations and ideas and make some grammatical changes. Then I write it over again, making more changes as I go. Sometimes I complete the whole process in an hour or two. Sometimes it takes a week or more.
- I like to do my first draft on paper—that is, after I've daydreamed for an hour or two, raided the refrigerator, and made a fresh pot of coffee. I specialise in procrastination. After running out of ways to distract myself, I start to scribble down everything I can think of. And I mean scribble—write fast, make a mess. When I figure out what I've scrawled, I try to fix it up into an orderly, halfway-decent essay. Then I put it aside (after

making another trip to the refrigerator) and start al over again. When I'm done, I compare both papers and combine them by taking some things out anc putting other things in. Then I read my draft out loud. If it sounds okay, I go to the computer and type it up.

— In trying to put together a paper, I go through four phases. First, there's the idea phase, where I get this bright idea. Then there is the productive phase, where I'm really smoking, and I start thinking about the Pulitzer Prize. After that, of course, comes the block phase, and all those prize-winning dreams turn into nightmares of this big, six-foot guy jammed into a first-grader's desk and being made to print the alphabet over and over again. Eventually (hours, sometimes days later), I hit the deadline phase: I realise that this sucker has got to be written, and so I start burning it out again. This phase often doesn't start until ten minutes before a paper is due, which doesn't leave a lot of time to proofread—a phase I never seem to get around to.

As these examples show, no single method of writing is followed by all writers in all circumstances. Each of us has to discover the approach that works best on any particular occasion. We can, however, identify four basic steps that most successful writers follow in one way or another:

1. *Discovering*: Finding a topic and coming up with something to say about it. A few of the discovery strategies that can help us to get started are freewriting, probing, and brainstorming.
2. *Drafting*: Putting ideas down in some rough form. A first draft is generally messy and repetitive and full of mistakes—and that's just fine. The purpose of a rough draft is to capture ideas and supporting

details, not compose a perfect paragraph or essay on the first attempt.

3. *Revising*: Changing and rewriting a draft to make it better. In this step, we respond to the needs of our readers by rearranging ideas and reshaping sentences to make clearer connections.
4. *Editing and Proofreading:* Carefully examining a paper to see that it contains no errors of grammar, spelling, or punctuation.

The four stages overlap, and at times we may have to back up and repeat a stage, but that doesn't mean we have to focus on all four stages at the same time. In fact, trying to do too much at one time is likely to create frustration, not make the writing go faster or easier.

In a paragraph or two, describe your own writing process—the steps that you ordinarily follow when composing a paper. How do you get started? Do you write several drafts or just one? If you revise, what sort of things do you look for and what sort of changes do you tend to make? How do you edit and proofread, and what types of errors do you most often find? Save this description when you're done, and then look at it again in a month or so to see what changes you have made in the way you write.

Paragraph Writing

The fundamental unit of composition is the paragraph. A paragraph consists of several sentences that are grouped together. This group of sentences together discuss one main subject. In formal academic English, paragraphs have three principal parts. These three parts are the topic sentence, body sentences, and the concluding sentence. We will also talk briefly about details in paragraphs.

The Topic Sentence

A topic sentence usually comes at the beginning of a paragraph; that is, it is usually the first sentence in a formal academic paragraph.

The topic sentence introduces the main idea of the paragraph. Summarise the main idea of your paragraph. Indicate to the reader what your paragraph will be about.

Example:

There are three reasons why Canada is one of the best countries in the world. First, Canada has an excellent health care system. All Canadians have access to medical services at a reasonable price. Second, Canada has a high standard of education. Students are taught by well-trained teachers and are encouraged to continue studying at university. Finally, Canada's cities are clean and efficiently managed. Canadian cities have many parks and lots of space for people to live. As a result, Canada is a desirable place to live.

Supporting Sentences

They come after the topic sentence, making up the body of a paragraph. They give details to develop and support the main idea of the paragraph. You should give supporting facts, details, and examples.

Example:

There are three reasons why Canada is one of the best countries in the world. *First, Canada has an excellent health care system. All Canadians have access to medical services at a reasonable price. Second, Canada has a high standard of education. Students are taught by well-trained teachers and are encouraged to continue studying at university. Finally, Canada's cities are clean and efficiently managed. Canadian cities have many parks and lots of space for people to live.* As a result, Canada is a desirable place to live.

Closing Sentence

The closing sentence is the last sentence in a paragraph. It restates the main idea of your paragraph. Restate the main idea of the paragraph using different words.
Example:

> There are three reasons why Canada is one of the best countries in the world. First, Canada has an excellent health care system. All Canadians have access to medical services at a reasonable price. Second, Canada has a high standard of education. Students are taught by well-trained teachers and are encouraged to continue studying at university. Finally, Canada's cities are clean and efficiently managed. Canadian cities have many parks and lots of space for people to live. *As a result, Canada is a desirable place to live.*

Pre-writing Paragraphs

The pre-writing stage is when you think carefully and organise your ideas for your paragraph before you begin writing.

Six pre-writing steps:

1. *Think carefully about what you are going to write. Ask yourself:* What question am I going to answer in this paragraph or essay? How can I best answer this question? What is the most important part of my answer? How can I make an introductory sentence (or thesis statement) from the most important part of my answer? What facts or ideas can I use to support my introductory sentence? How can I make this paragraph or essay interesting? Do I need more facts on this topic? Where can I find more facts on this topic?
2. *Open your notebook.* Write out your answers to the above questions. You do not need to spend a lot of time doing this; just write enough to help you

remember why and how you are going to write your paragraph or essay.

3. *Collect facts related to your paragraph or essay topic.* Look for and write down facts that will help you to answer your question. Timesaving hint: make sure the facts you are writing are related to the exact question you are going to answer in your paragraph or essay.
4. *Write down your own ideas.* Ask yourself: What else do I want to say about this topic? Why should people be interested in this topic? Why is this topic important?
5. *Find the main idea of your paragraph or essay.* Choose the most important point you are going to present. If you cannot decide which point is the most important, just choose one point and stick to it throughout your paragraph or essay.
6. *Organise your facts and ideas in a way that develops your main idea.* Once you have chosen the most important point of your paragraph or essay, you must find the best way to tell your reader about it. Look at the facts you have written. Look at your own ideas on the topic. Decide which facts and ideas will best support the main idea of your paragraph. Once you have chosen the facts and ideas you plan to use, ask yourself which order to put them in the paragraph. Write down your own note set that you can use to guide yourself as you write your paragraph or essay.

Writing Steps

The writing stage is when you turn your ideas into sentences. Here is some steps:

1. Open your notebook and word processor.

2. Write the topic sentence, supporting sentences, and closing sentence.
3. Write clear and simple sentences to express your meaning.
4. Focus on the main idea of your paragraph.
5. Use the dictionary to help you find additional words to express your ideas.

Editing Stage

The editing stage is when you check your paragraph for mistakes and correct them.

Grammar and Spelling

1. Check your spelling.
2. Check your grammar.
3. Read your essay again.
4. Make sure each sentence has a subject.
5. See if your subjects and verbs agree with each other.
6. Check the verb tenses of each sentence.
7. Make sure that each sentence makes sense.

Style and Organisation

1. Make sure your paragraph has a topic sentence.
2. Make sure your supporting sentences focus on the main idea.
3. Make sure you have a closing sentence.
4. Check that all your sentences focus on the main idea.
5. See if your paragraph is interesting.

Essay Writing

An essay can have many purposes, but the basic structure is the same no matter what. You may be writing an essay to argue for a particular point of view or to explain the steps necessary to complete a task.

Either way, your essay will have the same basic format.

If you follow a few simple steps, you will find that the essay almost writes itself. You will be responsible only for supplying ideas, which are the important part of the essay anyway.

These simple steps will guide you through the essay writing process:

1. Decide on your topic.
2. Prepare an outline or diagram of your ideas.
3. Write your thesis statement.
4. Write the body.
   (*a*) Write the main points.
   (*b*) Write the subpoints.
   (*c*) Elaborate on the subpoints.
5. Write the introduction.
6. Write the conclusion.
7. Add the finishing touches.

Decide on Your Topic

You may have no choice as to your topic. If this is the case, you still may not be ready to jump to the next step.

Think about the type of paper you are expected to produce. Should it be a general overview, or a specific analysis of the topic? If it should be an overview, then you are probably ready to move to the next step. If it should be a specific analysis, make sure your topic is fairly specific. If it is too general, you must choose a narrower subtopic to discuss.

For example, the topic "India" is a general one. If your objective is to write an overview, this topic is suitable. If your objective is to write a specific analysis, this topic is too general. You must narrow it to something like "Politics in India" or "India's Culture."

Once you have determined that your topic will be suitable, you can move on.

If you have not been assigned a topic, then the whole world lies before you. Sometimes that seems to make the task of starting even more intimidating. Actually, this means that you are free to choose a topic of interest to you, which will often make your essay a stronger one.

Define Your Purpose

The first thing you must do is think about the purpose of the essay you must write. Is your purpose to persuade people to believe as you do, to explain to people how to complete a particular task, to educate people about some person, place, thing or idea, or something else entirely? Whatever topic you choose must fit that purpose.

Brainstorm Subjects of Interest

Once you have determined the purpose of your essay, write down some subjects that interest you. No matter what the purpose of your essay is, an endless number of topics will be suitable.

If you have trouble thinking of subjects, start by looking around you. Is there anything in your surroundings that interests you? Think about your life. What occupies most of your time? That might make for a good topic. Don't evaluate the subjects yet; just write down anything that springs to mind.

Evaluate Each Initial Topic

If you can think of at least a few topics that would be appropriate, you must simply consider each one individually. Think about how you feel about that topic. If you must educate, be sure it is a subject about which you are particularly well-informed. If you must persuade, be sure it is a subject about which you are at least moderately passionate. Of course, the most important factor in choosing a topic is the number of ideas you have about that topic.

Even if none of the subjects you thought of seem particularly appealing, try just choosing one to work with. It may turn out to be a better topic than you at first thought.

Before you are ready to move on in the essay-writing process, look one more time at the topic you have selected. Think about the type of paper you are expected to produce. Should it be a general overview, or a specific analysis of the topic? If it should be an overview, then you are probably ready to move to the next step. If it should be a specific analysis, make sure your topic is fairly specific. If it is too general, you must choose a narrower subtopic to discuss.

Once you have determined that your topic will be suitable, you can move on.

Organise Your Ideas

The purpose of an outline or diagram is to put your ideas about the topic on paper, in a moderately organised format. The structure you create here may still change before the essay is complete, so don't agonise over this.

Decide whether you prefer the cut-and-dried structure of an outline or a more flowing structure. If you start one or the other and decide it isn't working for you, you can always switch later.

Diagram

1. Begin your diagram with a circle or a horizontal line or whatever shape you prefer in the middle of the page.
2. Inside the shape or on the line, write your topic.
3. From your centre shape or line, draw three or four lines out into the page. Be sure to spread them out.
4. At the end of each of these lines, draw another circle or horizontal line or whatever you drew in the centre of the page.
5. In each shape or on each line, write the main ideas that you have about your topic, or the main points that you want to make.
   (a) If you are trying to persuade, you want to write your best arguments.
   (b) If you are trying to explain a process, you want to write the steps that should be followed.
   (c) You will probably need to group these into categories.
   (d) If you have trouble grouping the steps into categories, try using Beginning, Middle, and End.
   (e) If you are trying to inform, you want to write the major categories into which your information can be divided.
6. From each of your main ideas, draw three or four lines out into the page.

7. At the end of each of these lines, draw another circle or horizontal line or whatever you drew in the centre of the page.
8. In each shape or on each line, write the facts or information that support that main idea.

When you have finished, you have the basic structure for your essay and are ready to continue.

Outline

1. Begin your outline by writing your topic at the top of the page.
2. Next, write the Roman numerals I, II, and III, spread apart down the left side of the page.
3. Next to each Roman numeral, write the main ideas that you have about your topic, or the main points that you want to make.
   - *(a)* If you are trying to persuade, you want to write your best arguments.
   - *(b)* If you are trying to explain a process, you want to write the steps that should be followed.
   - *(c)* You will probably need to group these into categories.
   - *(d)* If you have trouble grouping the steps into categories, try using Beginning, Middle, and End.
   - *(e)* If you are trying to inform, you want to write the major categories into which your information can be divided.
4. Under each Roman numeral, write A, B, and C down the left side of the page.
5. Next to each letter, write the facts or information that support that main idea.

When you have finished, you have the basic structure for your essay and are ready to continue.

Compose a Thesis Statement

Now that you have decided, at least tentatively, what information you plan to present in your essay, you are ready to write your thesis statement.

The thesis statement tells the reader what the essay will be about, and what point you, the author, will be making. You know what the essay will be about. That was your topic. Now you must look at your outline or diagram and decide what point you will be making. What do the main ideas and supporting ideas that you listed say about your topic?

Your thesis statement will have two parts.

1. The first part states the topic.
   - *(a)* India's Culture
   - *(b)* Building a Model Train Set
   - *(c)* Public Transportation
2. The second part states the point of the essay.
   - *(a)* has a rich and varied history
   - *(b)* takes time and patience
   - *(c)* can solve some of our city's most persistent and pressing problems

   Or in the second part you could simply list the three main ideas you will discuss.
   - *(a)* has a long history, blends traditions from several other cultures, and provides a rich heritage.
   - *(b)* requires an investment in time, patience, and materials.

(c) helps with traffic congestion, resource management, and the city budget.

Once you have formulated a thesis statement that fits this pattern and with which you are comfortable, you are ready to continue.

Write the Body Paragraphs

In the body of the essay, all the preparation up to this point comes to fruition. The topic you have chosen must now be explained, described, or argued.

Each main idea that you wrote down in your diagram or outline will become one of the body paragraphs. If you had three or four main ideas, you will have three or four body paragraphs.

Each body paragraph will have the same basic structure.

1. Start by writing down one of your main ideas, in sentence form. If your main idea is "reduces freeway congestion," you might say this: Public transportation reduces freeway congestion.
2. Next, write down each of your supporting points for that main idea, but leave four or five lines in between each point.
3. In the space under each point, write down some elaboration for that point.

   Elaboration can be further description or explanation or discussion.

   Supporting Point. Commuters appreciate the cost savings of taking public transportation rather than driving.

   Less driving time means less maintenance expense, such as oil changes. Of course, less driving time means savings on gasoline as well. In many cases, these savings amount to more than the cost of riding public transportation.

4. If you wish, include a summary sentence for each paragraph.
5. This is not generally needed, however, and such sentences have a tendency to sound stilted, so be cautious about using them.

Once you have fleshed out each of your body paragraphs, one for each main point, you are ready to continue.

Write the Introduction

Your essay lacks only two paragraphs now: the introduction and the conclusion. These paragraphs will give the reader a point of entry to and a point of exit from your essay.

The introduction should be designed to attract the reader's attention and give her an idea of the essay's focus.

1. *Begin with an attention grabber*. The attention grabber you use is up to you, but here are some ideas:
   - *(a)* Startling information.
   - *(b)* This information must be true and verifiable, and it doesn't need to be totally new to your readers. It could simply be a pertinent fact that explicitly illustrates the point you wish to make.
   - *(c)* If you use a piece of startling information, follow it with a sentence or two of elaboration.
   - *(d)* Anecdote.

     An anecdote is a story that illustrates a point.

     Be sure your anecdote is short, to the point, and relevant to your topic. This can be a very effective opener for your essay, but use it carefully.

(e) Dialogue.

An appropriate dialogue does not have to identify the speakers, but the reader must understand the point you are trying to convey. Use only two or three exchanges between speakers to make your point.

Follow dialogue with a sentence or two of elaboration.

(f) Summary Information.

A few sentences explaining your topic in general terms can lead the reader gently to your thesis. Each sentence should become gradually more specific, until you reach your thesis.

2. If the attention grabber was only a sentence or two, add one or two more sentences that will lead the reader from your opening to your thesis statement.
3. Finish the paragraph with your thesis statement.

Writing Conclusion

The conclusion brings closure to the reader, summing up your points or providing a final perspective on your topic. All the conclusion needs is three or four strong sentences which do not need to follow any set formula. Simply review the main points or briefly describe your feelings about the topic. Even an anecdote can end your essay in a useful way.

Add the Finishing Touches

You have now completed all of the paragraphs of your essay. Before you can consider this a finished product, however, you must give some thought to the formatting of your paper.

Check the Order of Your Paragraphs

Look at your paragraphs. Which one is the strongest? You might want to start with the strongest paragraph, end with the second strongest, and put the weakest in the middle. Whatever order you decide on, be sure it makes sense. If your paper is describing a process, you will probably need to stick to the order in which the steps must be completed.

Check the Instructions for the Assignment

When you prepare a final draft, you must be sure to follow all of the instructions you have been given.

- Are your margins correct?
- Have you titled it as directed?
- What other information (name, date, etc.) must you include?
- Did you double-space your lines?

Check Your Writing

Nothing can substitute for revision of your work. By reviewing what you have done, you can improve weak points that otherwise would be missed. Read and reread your paper.

- Does it make logical sense?
- Leave it for a few hours and then read it again. Does it still make logical sense?
- Do the sentences flow smoothly from one another?
- If not, try to add some words and phrases to help connect them. Transition words, such as "therefore" or "however," sometimes help. Also, you might refer in one sentence to a thought in the previous sentence. This is especially useful when you move from one paragraph to another.

– Have you run a spell checker or a grammar checker?
– These aids cannot catch every error, but they might catch errors that you have missed.

KEYS OF EFFECTIVE WRITING

Writing is a form of communication between two or more people. Unclear writing may lead to misunderstanding by the reader. Unclear writing reflects negatively on the writer and sometimes reflects foggy thinking. Being able to write clearly strengthens the writer's self-esteem.

Writing is a transaction between the writer and the reader, with the primary obligation for conveying the message accurately and understandably being on the writer.

The spoken language is looser than the written language, as facial expression, gestures, pointing, etc. cannot be included in the written document.

Whatever the message, it can be transmitted to the reader via the written word, though much effort is required if complicated messages are conveyed clearly.

We seldom recognise how poorly we write, because we know what we intended to say and are likely to mistakenly believe that our written passage actually communicates that message.

A clear sentence is no accident, as so many little things can lead to misinterpretation. Almost always, with more time and effort we could improve our writing, often—though not always—by reduction in wording. Writing is a craft that can be improved, principally by observing carefully others' writing and by practising one's own writing.

Characteristics of Effective Writing

- *Accurate and objective*: It is factual and uninfluenced by emotion or prejudice.
- *Clear and coherent*. It can be understood and cannot be misunderstood.
- *Simple and economical*. It says only what needs to be said.
- *Cohesive*. It sticks together because every sentence and every word contributes to the central idea and not merely to each other.

Suggestions on Writing Accurately and Objectively:

- Observe carefully and record and describe precisely.
- Use correct grammar and punctuation.
- Use adverbs cautiously. Guard against using too many and be careful about their location. For example: He is the only one I like///He is the one only I like.
- Avoid excessive and inappropriate use of jargon and cliches.
- Use value-laden and opinion words cautiously (e.g., surely, unquestionably).
- Include contradictory evidence when appropriate.

Suggestions on Writing Clearly and Coherently:

- Omit no key words.

  Incorrect: The film container is your first step.

  Correct: Opening the film container is your first step.
- Avoid ambiguity.

Incorrect: Uncle John went to feed the cow with an umbrella.

— Avoid overstuffing sentences.

Incorrect: For non-smokers, a smoke filled room causes not only teary eyes and runny noses but also can alter auditory and visual perceptions as well, which is irritating but not associated with any serious disease, except for people with heart and lung ailments who are threatened with major problems from smoke.

— Avoid multi-noun modifiers (noun strings).

Incorrect: Diabetic patient blood pressure reduction may be a consequence of renal extract depressor agent application.

— Place key words or phrases at either the beginning or the end of the sentence.

Correct: I expect a refund because of your error in my laboratory test.

Correct: Because of your error in my laboratory test, I expect a refund.

— Use active voice (forceful verbs) when possible.

Incorrect: Attempts were made on the part of the engineering staff in regard to an assessment of the project.

Suggestions on Writing Simply and Economically:

— *Use uncomplicated sentences.*

Example 1: The strength that the elephant has is amazing.

Example 2: The strength of the elephant is amazing.

Example 3: The elephant's strength is amazing.

— *Avoid long introductory phrases.*

Example: For all intents and purposes, few women have yet achieved equal pay for equal work. Improvement: Few women have yet achieved equal pay for equal work.

— *Use plain words.*

Bad: The recent drug thefts have necessitated stronger security measures.

Good: The recent drug thefts have made it necessary for stronger security measures.

— *Use numbers to indicate points.*

Example: Our present careless use of coal and oil will lead to a series of unpleasant events: *(a)* all of us will have to cut back drastically on our use of resources; *(b)* only the rich will be able to afford the resources; and *(c)* all access to the resources will end by the turn of the century because the resources will be depleted.

— *Do not qualify words that have only one meaning.*

Incorrect: Several positive benefits may result from this new innovation.

— *Avoid needless repetition.*

Incorrect: Breathing is restored by artificial respiration. Artificial respiration means that breathing is being maintained by artificial means. Techniques of artificial respiration are mouth-to-mouth and mouth-to-nose. Artificial respiration must always be performed when external cardiac massage is being done.

— *Use active voice when possible.*

— *Be concise in word usage.*

Incorrect: On account of the fact that the fire had spread to two floors, all stairwells were sealed off.

Correct: Because the fire had spread to two floors, all stairwells were sealed off.

Suggestions on Writing Cohesively:

- Clearly state the central idea (topic sentence).
- Stick to the topic.
- Leave out irrelevant details.
- Organise sentences in a meaningful manner. Spatial (from one physical location to another); chronological; example (topic sentence supported by examples); reasoning (viewpoint supported by reasons); cause/effect; effect/cause; comparison/contrast.

4

Writing with Style

From the Latin word stylus, "a pointed instrument used for writing." That, according to our glossary entry, is what the word style meant 2,000 years ago. Nowadays, definitions of style point not to the instrument used by the writer but to characteristics of the writing itself:

The way in which something is said, done, expressed, or performed: a style of speech and writing. Narrowly interpreted as those figures that ornament discourse; broadly, as representing a manifestation of the person speaking or writing. All figures of speech fall within the domain of style.

It is the object of every writer to put his thoughts into as effective form as possible so as to make a good impression on the reader. A person may have noble thoughts and ideas but be unable to express them in such a way as to appeal to others, consequently he cannot exert the full force of his intellectuality nor leave the imprint of his character upon his time, whereas many a man but indifferently gifted may wield such a facile pen as to attract attention and win for himself an envious place among his contemporaries.

In everyday life one sees illustrations of men of excellent mentality being cast aside and ones of mediocre or in some cases, little, if any, ability chosen to fill important places. The former are unable to impress their personality; they have great thoughts, great ideas, but these thoughts and ideas are locked up in their brains and are like prisoners behind the bars struggling to get free. The key of language which would open the door is wanting, hence they have to remain locked up.

Many a man has to pass through the world unheard of and of little benefit to it or himself, simply because he cannot bring out what is in him and make it subservient to his will. It is the duty of every one to develop his best, not only for the benefit of himself but for the good of his fellow men. It is not at all necessary to have great learning or acquirements, the labourer is as useful in his own place as the philosopher in his; nor is it necessary to have many talents.

One talent rightly used is much better than ten wrongly used. Often a man can do more with one than his contemporary can do with ten, often a man can make one dollar go farther than twenty in the hands of his neighbour, often the poor man lives more comfortably than the millionaire. All depends upon the individual himself. If he make right use of what the Creator has given him and live according to the laws of God and nature he is fulfilling his allotted place in the universal scheme of creation, in other words, when he does his best, he is living up to the standard of a useful manhood.

Now in order to do his best a man of ordinary intelligence and education should be able to express himself correctly both in speaking and writing, that is, he should be able to convey his thoughts in an intelligent manner which the simplest can understand. The manner in which a speaker or writer conveys his thoughts is known as his Style.

In other words *Style* may be defined as the peculiar manner in which a man expresses his conceptions through the medium of language. It depends upon the choice of words and their arrangement to convey a meaning. Scarcely any two writers have exactly the same style, that is to say, express their ideas after the same peculiar form, just as no two mortals are fashioned by nature in the same mould, so that one is an exact counterpart of the other.

Just as men differ in the accent and tones of their voices, so do they differ in the construction of their language.

Two reporters sent out on the same mission, say to report a fire, will verbaliy differ in their accounts though materially both descriptions will be the same as far as the leading facts are concerned. One will express himself in a style *different* from the other.

If you are asked to describe the dancing of a red-haired lady at the last charity ball you can either say– "The ruby Circe, with the Titian locks glowing like the oriflamme which surrounds the golden god of day as he sinks to rest amid the crimson glory of the burnished West, gave a divine exhibition of the Terpsichorean art which thrilled the souls of the multitude" or, you can simply say– "The red-haired lady danced very well and pleased the audience."

The former is a specimen of the ultra florid or bombastic style which may be said to depend upon the pomposity of verbosity for its effect, the latter is a specimen of simple *natural* Style. Needless to say it is to be preferred. The other should be avoided. It stamps the writer as a person of shallowness, ignorance and inexperience. It has been eliminated from the newspapers. Even the most flatulent of yellow sheets no longer tolerate it in their columns. Affectation and pedantry in style are now universally condemned.

It is the duty of every speaker and writer to labour after a pleasing style. It gains him an entrance where he would otherwise be debarred. Often the interest of a subject depends as much on the way it is presented as on the subject itself. One writer will make it attractive, another repulsive. For instance take a passage in history. Treated by one historian it is like a desiccated mummy, dry, dull, disgusting, while under the spell of another it is, as it were, galvanised into a virile living thing which not only pleases but captivates the reader.

Diction

The first requisite of style is *choice* of *words*, and this comes under the head of *Diction*, the property of style which has reference to the words and phrases used in speaking and writing. The secret of literary skill from any standpoint consists in putting the right word in the right place. In order to do this it is imperative to know the meaning of the words we use, their exact literal meaning. Many synonymous words are seemingly interchangeable and appear as if the same meaning were applicable to three or four of them at the same time, but when all such words are reduced to a final analysis it is clearly seen that there is a marked difference in their meaning. For instance *grief* and *sorrow* seem to be identical, but they are not. *Grief* is active, *sorrow* is more or less passive; *grief* is caused by troubles and misfortunes which come to us from the outside, while *sorrow* is often the consequence of our own acts. *Grief* is frequently loud and violent, *sorrow* is always quiet and retiring. *Grief* shouts, *Sorrow* remains calm.

If you are not sure of the exact meaning of a word look it up immediately in the dictionary. Sometimes some of our great scholars are puzzled over simple words in regard to meaning, spelling or pronunciation. Whenever you meet a strange word note it down until you discover its meaning and use. Read the best books you can get, books written by men and women who are acknowledged masters of language, and study how they use their words, where they place them in the sentences, and the meanings they convey to the readers.

Mix in good society. Listen attentively to good talkers and try to imitate their manner of expression. If a word is used you do not understand, don't be ashamed to ask its meaning.

True, a small vocabulary will carry you through, but it is an advantage to have a large one. When you live alone a little pot serves just as well as a large one to cook your victuals and it is handy and convenient, but when your friends or neighbours come to dine with you, you will need a much larger pot and it is better to have it in store, so that you will not be put to shame for your scantiness of furnishings.

Get as many words as you possibly can–if you don't need them now, pack them away in the garrets of your brain so that you can call upon them if you require them.

Keep a note book, jot down the words you don't understand or clearly understand and consult the dictionary when you get time.

PURITY

Purity of style consists in using words which are reputable, national and present, which means that the words are in current use by the best authorities, that they are used throughout the nation and not confined to one particular part, and that they are words in constant use at the present time.

There are two guiding principles in the choice of words–*good use* and *good taste. Good use* tells us whether a word is right or wrong; *good taste,* whether it is adapted to our purpose or not.

A word that is obsolete or too new to have gained a place in the language, or that is a provincialism, should not be used.

Here are the ten commandments of English style:

1. Do not use foreign words.
2. Do not use a long word when a short one will serve your purpose. *Fire* is much better than *conflagration.*
3. Do not use technical words, or those understood only by specialists in their respective lines, except when you are writing especially for such people.
4. Do not use slang.
5. Do not use provincialisms, as "I guess" for "I think"; "I reckon" for "I know," etc.
6. Do not in writing prose, use poetical or antiquated words: as "lore, e'er, morn, yea, nay, verily, peradventure."
7. Do not use trite and hackneyed words and expressions; as, "on the job," "up and in"; "down and out."
8. Do not use newspaper words which have not established a place in the language as "to bugle"; "to suicide," etc.
9. Do not use ungrammatical words and forms; as, "I am't;" "he don't."
10. Do not use ambiguous words or phrases; as– "He showed me all about the house."

Trite words, similes and metaphors which have become hackneyed and worn out should be allowed to rest in the oblivion of past usage. Such expressions and phrases as

"Sweet sixteen" "the Almighty Money," "Uncle Sam," "On the fence," "The Glorious Fourth," "Young America," "The lords of creation," "The rising generation," "The weaker sex," "The weaker vessel," "Sweetness long drawn out" and "chief cook and bottle washer," should be put on the shelf as they are utterly worn out from too much usage.

Some of the old similes which have outlived their usefulness and should be pensioned off, are "Sweet as sugar," "Bold as a lion," "Strong as an ox," "Quick as a flash," "Cold as ice," "Stiff as a poker," "White as snow," "Busy as a bee," "Pale as a ghost," "Rich as Croesus," "Cross as a bear" and a great many more far too numerous to mention.

Be as original as possible in the use of expression. Don't follow in the old rut but try and strike out for yourself. This does not mean that you should try to set the style, or do anything outlandish or out of the way, or be an innovator on the prevailing custom. In order to be original there is no necessity for you to introduce something novel or establish a precedent.

The probability is you are not fit to do either, by education or talent. While following the style of those who are acknowledged leaders you can be original in your language. Try and clothe an idea different from what it has been clothed and better. If you are speaking or writing of dancing don't talk or write about "tripping the light fantastic toe." It is over two hundred years since Milton expressed it that way in 'L'Allegro." You're not a Milton and besides over a million have stolen it from Milton until it is now no longer worth stealing.

Don't resurrect obsolete words such as *whilom, yclept, wis,* etc., and be careful in regard to obsolescent words, that is, words that are at the present time gradually passing from use such as *quoth, trow, betwixt, amongst, froward,* etc.

Beware of new words. Be original in the construction and arrangement of your language, but don't try to originate words. Leave that to the Masters of language, and don't be the first to try such words, wait until the chemists of speech have tested them and passed upon their merits.

Propriety

Propriety of style consists in using words in their proper sense and as in the case of purity, good usage is the principal test. Many words have acquired in actual use a meaning very different from what they once possessed. "Prevent" formerly meant to go before, and that meaning is implied in its Latin derivation. Now it means to put a stop to, to hinder. To attain propriety of style it is necessary to avoid confounding words derived from the same root; as *respectfully* and *respectively;* it is necessary to use words in their accepted sense or the sense which everyday use sanctions.

Simplicity

Simplicity of style has reference to the choice of simple words and their unaffected presentation. Simple words should always be used in preference to compound, and complicated ones when they express the same or almost the same meaning. The Anglo-Saxon element in our language comprises the simple words which express the relations of everyday life, strong, terse, vigorous, the language of the fireside, street, market and farm. It is this style which characterises the Bible and many of the great English classics such as the "Pilgrim's Progress," "Robinson Crusoe," and "Gulliver's Travels."

Clearness

Clearness of style should be one of the leading considerations with the beginner in composition. He must avoid all obscurity and ambiguous phrases. If he write a sentence or phrase and see that a meaning might be inferred from it otherwise than intended, he should re-write it in such a way that there can be no possible doubt. Words, phrases or clauses that are closely related should be placed as near to each other as possible that their mutual relation may clearly appear, and no word should be omitted that is necessary to the complete expression of thought.

Unity

Unity is that property of style which keeps all parts of a sentence in connection with the principal thought and logically subordinate to it. A sentence may be constructed as to suggest the idea of oneness to the mind, or it may be so loosely put together as to produce a confused and indefinite impression. Ideas that have but little connection should be expressed in separate sentences, and not crowded into one. Keep long parentheses out of the middle of your sentences and when you have apparently brought your sentences to a close don't try to continue the thought or idea by adding supplementary clauses.

Strength

Strength is that property of style which gives animation, energy and vivacity to language and sustains the interest of the reader. It is as necessary to language as good food is to the body. Without it the words are weak and feeble and create little or no impression on the mind. In order to have strength the language must be concise, that is, much expressed in little compass, you must hit the nail fairly on the head and drive it in straight. Go critically over what you write and strike out every word, phrase and clause the omission of which impairs neither the clearness nor force of the sentence and so avoid redundancy, tautology and circumlocution. Give the most important words the most prominent places, which, as has been pointed out elsewhere, are the beginning and end of the sentence.

Harmony

Harmony is that property of style which gives a smoothness to the sentence, so that when the words are sounded their connection becomes pleasing to the ear. It adapts sound to sense. Most people construct their sentences without giving thought to the way they will sound and as a consequence we have many jarring and discordant combinations such as "Thou strengthenedst thy position and actedst arbitrarily and derogatorily to my interests."

Harsh, disagreeable verbs are liable to occur with the Quaker form *Thou* of the personal pronoun. This form is now nearly obsolete, the plural *you* being almost universally used. To obtain harmony in the sentence long words that are hard to pronounce and combinations of letters of one kind should be avoided.

Expressive of Writer

Style is expressive of the writer, as to who he is and what he is. As a matter of structure in composition it is the indication of what a man can do; as a matter of quality it is an indication of what he is.

Kinds of Style

Style has been classified in different ways, but it admits of so many designations that it is very hard to enumerate a table. In fact there are as many styles as there are writers, for no two authors write *exactly after* the same form. However, we may classify the styles of the various authors in broad divisions as *(a)* dry, *(b)* plain, *(c)* neat, *(d)* elegant, *(e)* florid, *(f)* bombastic.

The *dry* style excludes all ornament and makes no effort to appeal to any sense of beauty. Its object is simply to express the thoughts in a correct manner. This style is exemplified by Berkeley.

The *plain* style does not seek ornamentation either, but aims to make clear and concise statements without any elaboration or embellishment. Locke and Whately illustrate the plain style.

The *neat* style only aspires after ornament sparingly. Its object is to have correct figures, pure diction and clear and harmonious sentences. Goldsmith and Gray are the acknowledged leaders in this kind of style.

The *elegant* style uses every ornament that can beautify and avoids every excess which would degrade. Macaulay and Addison have been enthroned as the kings of this style. To them all writers bend the knee in homage.

The *florid* style goes to excess in superfluous and superficial ornamentation and strains after a highly coloured imagery. The poems of Ossian typify this style.

The *bombastic* is characterised by such an excess of words, figures and ornaments as to be ridiculous and disgusting. It is like a circus clown dressed up in gold tinsel Dickens gives a fine example of it in Sergeant Buzfuz' speech in the "Pickwick Papers." Among other varieties of style may be mentioned the colloquial, the laconic, the concise, the diffuse, the abrupt the flowing, the quaint, the epigrammatic, the flowery, the feeble, the nervous, the vehement, and the affected. The manner of these is sufficiently indicated by the adjective used to describe them.

In fact, style is as various as character and expresses the individuality of the writer, or in other words, as the French writer Buffon very aptly remarks, "the style is the man himself."

Using Figurative Style

Figures of speech is mode of expression in which words are used out of their literal meaning or out of their ordinary use in order to add beauty or emotional intensity or to transfer the poet's sense impressions by comparing or identifying one thing with another that has a meaning familiar to the reader. Some important figures of speech are: simile, metaphor, personification, hyperbole and symbol.

We use figures of speech in "figurative language" to add colour and interest, and to awaken the imagination. Figurative language is everywhere, from classical works like Shakespeare or the Bible, to everyday speech, pop music and television commercials. It makes the reader or listener use their imagination and understand much more than the plain words.

Figurative language is the opposite of literal language. Literal language means exactly what it says. Figurative language means something different to (and usually more than) what it says on the surface:

- He ran fast. (literal)
- He ran like the wind. (figurative)

In the above example "like the wind" is a figure of speech (in this case, a simile). It is important to recognise the difference between literal and figurative language. There are many figures of speech that are commonly used and which you can learn by heart. At other times, writers and speakers may invent their own figures of speech. If you do not recognise them as figures of speech and think that they are literal, you will find it difficult to understand the language.

As figurative language is to be met with in almost every sentence; and, when properly employed, confers beauty and strength on composition; some knowledge of it appears to be indispensable to the scholars, who are learning to form their sentences with perspicuity, accuracy, and force. We shall, therefore, enumerate the principal figures, and give them some explanation.

In general, Figures of Speech imply some departure from simplicity of expression; the idea which we mean to convey is expressed in a particular manner, and with some circumstance added, which is designed to render the impression more strong and vivid. When I say, for instance, "That a good man enjoys comfort in the midst of adversity"; I just express my thoughts in the simplest manner possible: but when I say, "To the upright there ariseth light in darkness"; the same sentiment is expressed in a figurative style; a new circumstance is introduced; "light," is put in the place of "comfort," and "darkness" is used to suggest the idea of "adversity."...

But, though figures imply a deviation from what may be reckoned the most simple form of speech, we are not thence to conclude, that they imply anything uncommon, or unnatural. On many occasions, they are both the most natural, and the most common method of uttering our sentiments. It would be very difficult to compose any discourse without using them often; nay, there are few sentences of considerable length, in which there does not occur some expression that may be termed a figure. This being the case, we may see the necessity of some attention, in order to understand their nature and use.

At the first rise of language, men would begin with giving names to the different objects which they discerned, or thought of. The stock of words would, then, be very small. As men's ideas multiplied, and their acquaintance with objects increased, their store of names and words would also increase. But to the vast variety of objects and ideas, no language is adequate. No language is so copious, as to have a separate word for every separate idea.

Men naturally sought to abridge this labour of multiplying words without end; and, in order to lay less burden on their memories, made one word, which they had already appropriated to a certain idea or object, stand also for some other idea or object, between which and the primary one, they found, or fancied, some relation. The names of sensible objects, were the words most early introduced; and were, by degrees, extended to those mental objects, of which men had more obscure conceptions, and to which they found it more difficult to assign distinct names. They borrowed, therefore, the name of some sensible idea, where their imagination found some affinity.

Thus, we speak of a piercing judgment, and a clear head; a soft or a hard heart; a rough or smooth behaviour. We say, inflamed by anger, warmed by love, swelled with pride, melted into grief; and these are almost the only significant words which we have for such ideas.

Figures make speech more effective, they beautify and emphasise it and give to it a relish and piquancy as salt does to food; besides they add energy and force to expression so that it irresistibly compels attention and interest. There are four kinds of figures, viz.:

1. *Figures of orthography* which change the spelling of a word;
2. *Figures of etymology* which change the form of words;

3. *Figures of Syntax* which change the construction of sentences;
4. *Figures of Rhetoric* or the art of speaking and writing effectively which change the mode of thought.

We shall only consider the last mentioned here as they are the most important, really giving to language the construction and style which make it a fitting medium for the intercommunication of ideas. Figures of Rhetoric have been variously classified, some authorities extending the list to a useless length. The fact is that any form of expression which conveys thought may be classified as a Figure.

The principal figures as well as the most important and those oftenest used are, Simile, Metaphor, Personification, Allegory, Synechdoche, Metonymy, Exclamation, Hyperbole, Apostrophe, Vision, Antithesis, Climax, Epigram, Interrogation and Irony. The first four are founded on resemblance, the second six on contiguity and the third five, on contrast.

In this chapter we will look at the common types of figure of speech.

Simile

A simile is a figure of speech that says that one thing is like another different thing. We can use similes to make descriptions more emphatic or vivid.

We often use the words as...as and like with similes.

Common patterns for similes, with example sentences, are:

— something [is*] AS adjective AS something

His skin was as cold as ice.

It felt as hard as rock.

She looked as gentle as a lamb.

– something [is*] like something

My love is like a red, red rose.

These cookies taste like garbage.

He had a temper (that was) like a volcano.

– something [does**] like something

He eats like a pig.

He smokes like a chimney.

They fought like cats and dogs.

* *stative verb: be, feel, smell, taste etc*

** *action verb*

Here are some more examples of well known similes:

[is] AS adjective AS something	*Meaning*
as blind as a bat	completely blind
as cold as ice	very cold
as flat as a pancake	completely flat
as gentle as a lamb	very gentle
as light as a feather	very light
as old as the hills	very old
as sharp as a knife	very sharp
as strong as a bull	very strong
as white as snow	pure white
as wise as an owl	very wise
[is] LIKE something	possible meaning (depending on context)
like a rose	beautiful
like a volcano	explosive
like garbage	disgusting
like an animal	inhuman
like spaghetti	entangled
like dewdrops	sweet and pure

like golddust	precious
like a tip	very untidy
like a dream	wonderful, incredible
like stars	bright and beautiful
[does] LIKE something	*meaning*
to drink like a fish	to drink a lot
to eat like a bird	to eat very little
to eat like a horse	to eat a lot
to eat like a pig	to eat impolitely
to fight like cats and dogs	to fight fiercely
to sing like an angel	to sing beautifully
to sleep like a log	to sleep well and soundly
to smoke like a chimney	to smoke heavily, all time
to soar like an eagle	to fly high and free
to work like a dog	to work very hard

Note that with the AS...AS pattern, the first AS is sometimes suppressed, for example:

– His skin was cold as ice.

The above patterns of simile are the most common, but there are others made with adverbs or words such as than and as if, for example:

– He ran as fast as the wind.

– He is larger than life.

– They ran as if for their lives.

Similes can include other figures of speech. For example, "He ran like greased lightning" is a simile that includes hyperbole (greased lightning).

Similes often make use of irony or sarcasm. In such cases they may even mean the opposite of the adjective used. Look at these examples:

– His explanation was as clear as mud. (not clear at all since mud is opaque)

— The film was about as interesting as watching a copy of Windows download. (long and boring)

Similes are often found (and they sometimes originate) in poetry and other literature. Here are a few examples:

— A woman without a man is like a fish without a bicycle—*Irina Dunn*

— Dawn breaks open like a wound that bleeds afresh—*Wilfred Owen*

— Death has many times invited me: it was like the salt invisible in the waves—*Pablo Neruda*

— Guiltless forever, like a tree—*Robert Browning*

— Happy as pigs in mud—*David Eddings*

— How like the winter hath my absence been—*William Shakespeare*

— As idle as a painted ship upon a painted ocean—*Samuel Taylor Coleridge*

— Jubilant as a flag unfurled—*Dorothy Parker*

Many similes are cliches (phrases that are overused and betray a lack of original thought). You should use well know similes with care, but it is certainly useful to know them so that you can understand language that contains them.

Metaphor

A metaphor is a figure of speech that says that one thing is another different thing. This allows us to use fewer words and forces the reader or listener to find the similarities. The word metaphor comes from the Greek word *metapherin* (meaning "transfer").

The simplest form of metaphor is: "The [first thing] is a [second thing]."Look at this example:

— Her *home* was a *prison*.

In the above sentence, we understand immediately that her home had some of the characteristics of a prison. Mainly, we imagine, she could not leave her home. She was trapped inside. Why it was a prison we do not know, but that would be clear from the context—perhaps her husband forced her to stay at home, perhaps she was afraid of the outside. We don't know, but the rest of the story would tell us.

What is important here is that in five simple words we understand a lot about her environment, how she felt and how she behaved. In this sentence, "prison" is a metaphor.

Look at another example:

– *Pinky* is a *sheep*.

What is one characteristic of sheep? They follow each other. So we can imagine that Pinky is a follower, not a leader. In this sentence "sheep" is a metaphor.

Metaphors are very common in everyday language. But poets also like to use metaphors. In the following famous verse (from *The Highwayman* by Alfred Noyes), can you spot three metaphors in the first three lines?

> The wind was a torrent of darkness among the gusty trees,
> The moon was a ghostly galleon tossed upon cloudy seas,
> The road was a ribbon of moonlight over the purple moor,
> And the highwayman came riding—
> Riding—riding—
> The highwayman came riding, up to the old inn-door.

Look at the examples of metaphors given in table of next page with sample sentences and meanings. All these metaphors are nouns. But there are other ways of making metaphors, for example with verbs or adjectives.

Metaphor example	Metaphorical sense	Original sense
I'm not an **angel**, but I wouldn't behave like that.	exemplary person	a spiritual being believed to be a messenger of God
America is a **melting pot**.	place where different peoples, styles and cultures are mixed together	a container in which metals or other materials are melted and mixed
John is a real **pig** when he eats.	greedy person	a four-legged animal kept for meat (pork)
My father is a **rock**.	very strong or reliable person	a hard, mineral material made of stone
How could she marry a **snake** like that!	traitor	a long, limbless reptile (eg: cobra, python, viper)
The policeman let him off with a **yellow card**.	warning	(in soccer) a yellow card that the referee shows to players when cautioning them

Metaphor example	Original sense of the word (example)
The committee **shot** her ideas **down** one by one.	Anti-aircraft guns shoot down planes.
The private detective **dug up** enough evidence to convince the police to act.	Dogs like to bury bones and dig them up later.
He **broke into** her conversation.	Burglars break into buildings.
The new movie was very popular. People **flocked** to see it.	Birds flock together before they migrate.
His head was **spinning** with ideas.	Some computer hard drives spin at over 10,000 revolutions per minute.
Reading that book **kindled** my interest in politics.	You need to start with twigs and small branches when you kindle a camp fire.
Tim lost his job after a **heated** argument with his boss.	We have a heated swimming pool.
The new car's **sexy** design increased sales for the company.	Some women think that lipstick makes them look sexy.
He was dressed rather vulgarly in a **loud** checked suit.	I can't hear you because the radio is too loud.
It wasn't long before their relationship turned **sour**.	Sour food has an acid taste like lemon or vinegar.

Difference Between Metaphor and Simile

Both similes and metaphors link one thing to another. A simile usually uses "as" or "like". A metaphor is a condensed simile, a shortcut to meaning, which omits "as" or "like." A metaphor creates a relationship directly and leaves more to the imagination. With simile A is *like* B. With metaphor A *is* B.

Simile	Metaphor
Your eyes are like the sun.	You are my sunshine.
He eats like a pig.	He is a pig.
He lives like a pig.	

In the phrase "to grasp the concept" the physical action "to grasp" is used as a metaphor for "to understand" (which is non-physical). But this phrase has been used so often that most English speakers do not have an image of the physical action in their mind. This metaphor has died; it is a "dead metaphor".

The awkward use of two or more different metaphors at the same time is normally best avoided. It creates conflicting images in the reader or listener's mind, reduces each metaphor's impact, and generally causes confusion. Look at this example:

— America is a *melting pot* where new ideas are *kindled*.

Hyperbole

Hyperbole is a figure of speech that uses an exaggerated or extravagant statement to create a strong emotional response. As a figure of speech it is not intended to be taken literally. Hyperbole is frequently used for humour. Examples of hyperbole are:

— They ran like greased lightning.

- He's got tons of money.
- Her brain is the size of a pea.
- He is older than the hills.
- I will die if she asks me to dance.
- She is as big as an elephant!
- I'm so hungry I could eat a horse.
- I have told you a million times not to lie!

The media and the advertising industry often use hyperbole (which may then be described as hype or media hype).

Oxymoron

An oxymoron is a figure of speech that deliberately uses two contradictory ideas. This contradiction creates a paradoxical image in the reader or listener's mind that generates a new concept or meaning for the whole. Some typical oxymorons are:

- A living death.
- Sometimes you have to be cruel to be kind.
- A deafening silence.
- Bitter-sweet.
- The Sounds of Silence (song title).
- Make haste slowly.
- He was conspicuous by his absence.

Pseudo Oxymorons

In the standard meaning of oxymoron the contradiction is deliberate. However, in popular usage oxymoron is sometimes used to mean "contradiction in terms", where the contradiction is unintentional. Such expressions, unlike real oxymorons, are commonly used without any sense of paradox in everyday language, for example:

- Anecdotal evidence.
- Friendly fire.
- Pretty ugly.

A common attempt at humour is to describe a certain phrase as an oxymoron, implying that the two parts of the phrase are mutually exclusive and that consequently the phrase as a whole must be nonsensical:

- Airline food.
- India culture.
- Eco-tourism.
- Computer security.
- Military intelligence.

Personification

Personification (from the Latin *persona,* person, and *facere,* to make) is the treating of an inanimate object as if it were animate and is probably the most beautiful and effective of all the figures.

> "The mountains sing together, the hills rejoice and clap their hands."
>
> "Earth felt the wound; and Nature from her seat,
> Sighing, through all her works, gave signs of woe."

Personification is the treating of an inanimate object as if it were animate and is probably the most beautiful and effective of all the figures of speech. Personification depends much on a vivid imagination and is adapted especially to poetical composition. It has two distinguishable forms:

- When personality is ascribed to the inanimate as in "The mountains sing together, the hills rejoice and clap their hands."

– When some quality of life is attributed to the inanimate; as, a raging storm; an angry sea; a whistling wind, etc.

Poems with personification examples can be found by the most famous poets including John Milton and Robert Frost.

– "Confusion heards his voice." from *Paradise Lost*—Book 3 by John Milton.
– Another example of personification from *Paradise Lost* by John Milton "Earth felt the wound; and Nature from her seat, Sighing, through all her works, gave signs of woe."
– *Spring Pools* by Robert Frost "And like the flowers beside them chill and shiver, Will like the flowers beside them soon be gone."

Examples of personification can be found in many examples of the poem, poems or poetry. Famous poets use this figure of speech to convey and emphasise unusual and vivid images. The use of strong word association changes the mode of thought and adds variation, embellishment and adornment to literary works.

In figurative language we use words in such a way that they differ somewhat from ordinary every-day speech and convey meanings in a more vivid and impressive manner. Figures, like personification make speech more effective, they beautify and emphasise it in Rhetoric which is the art of speaking and writing effectively. Figures of speech such as Personification use word association to convey emotion and mood often in a non-literal sense.

Figures of speech such as personification adds adornment, beautifies, colours, elegant variation, embellishment, embroidery, emphasis, exaggeration, exclamation, flourish, floweriness, irony, lushness and luxuriance to the English language.

Allegory

An Allegory (from the Greek *allos*, other, and *agoreuein*, to speak), is a form of expression in which the words are symbolical of something. It is very closely allied to the metaphor, in fact is a continued metaphor. Allegory, metaphor and simile have three points in common,—they are all founded on resemblance. "Ireland is like a thorn in the side of England;" this is simile. "Ireland is a thorn in the side of England;" this is metaphor. "Once a great giant sprang up out of the sea and lived on an island all by himself.

On looking around he discovered a little girl on another small island near by. He thought the little girl could be useful to him in many ways so he determined to make her subservient to his will. He commanded her, but she refused to obey, then he resorted to very harsh measures with the little girl, but she still remained obstinate and obdurate. He continued to oppress her until finally she rebelled and became as a thorn in his side to prick him for his evil attitude towards her;" this is an allegory in which the giant plainly represents England and the little girl, Ireland; the implication is manifest though no mention is made of either country.

Strange to say the most perfect allegory in the English language was written by an almost illiterate and ignorant man, and written too, in a dungeon cell. In the "Pilgrim's Progress," Bunyan, the itinerant tinker, has given us by far the best allegory ever penned. Another good one is "The Faerie Queen" by Edmund Spenser.

Synecdoche

Synecdoche is a figure of speech in which:

- A term denoting a part of something is used to refer to the whole thing (Pars pro toto), or
- A term denoting a thing (a "whole") is used to refer to part of it (Totum pro parte), or
- A term denoting a specific class of thing is used to refer to a larger, more general class, or
- A term denoting a general class of thing is used to refer to a smaller, more specific class (Bindo pro parte), or
- A term denoting a material is used to refer to an object composed of that material.

In figurative language we use words in such a way that they differ somewhat from ordinary every-day speech and convey meanings in a more vivid and impressive manner. Figures, like synecdoche make speech more effective, they beautify and emphasise it in Rhetoric which is the art of speaking and writing effectively. Figures of speech such as synecdoche use word association to convey emotion and mood often in a non-literal sense.

Synecdoche is closely related to metonymy (the figure of speech in which a term denoting one thing is used to refer to a related thing); indeed, synecdoche is sometimes considered a subclass of metonymy. It is more distantly related to other figures of speech, such as metaphor.

Examples of synecdoche can be found in many examples of the poem, poems or poetry. Famous poets use this figure of speech to convey and emphasise unusual and vivid images. The use of strong word association changes the mode of thought and adds variation, embellishment and adornment to literary works.

Poems with synecdoche examples can be found by the most famous poets including Shakespeare, Swift and Frost:

- "Friends, Romans, countrymen: lend me your ears"—*One of the most famous example of synecdoche by William Shakespeare.*
- "Prepar'd to scrub the entry and the stairs. The youth with broomy stumps began to trace"—*From 'A Description of the Morning' by Jonathan Swift (1667-1745) where the stump of the broom's straw stands in for the whole of the broom.*
- Stopping by Woods on a Snowy Evening—*by Robert Frost where the journey through woods and forests in the poem represent life's journey.*
- Tell that its sculptor well those passions read Which yet survive, stamped on these lifeless things, The hand that mocked them—*From "Ozymandias" by Shelley.*
- I should have been a pair of ragged claws Scuttling across the floors of silent seas—*T. S. Eliot, The Love Song of J. Alfred Prufrock.*

Metonymy

Metonymy (from the Greek *meta,* change, and *onyma,* a name) is the designation of an object by one of its accompaniments, in other words, it is a figure by which the name of one object is put for another when the two are so related that the mention of one readily suggests the other. Thus when we say of a drunkard–"He loves the bottle" we do not mean that he loves the glass receptacle, but the liquor that it is supposed to contain. Metonymy, generally speaking, has, three subdivisions:

1. When an effect is put for cause or vice versa: as 'Gray hairs should be respected," meaning old age. "He writes a fine hand," that is, handwriting.
2. When the sign is put for the thing signified; as, "The pen is mightier than the sword," meaning literary power is superior to military force.

3. When the container is put for the thing contained; as "The House was called to order," meaning the members in the House.

Examples of metonymy can be found in many examples of literature or poetry. The use of strong word association changes the mode of thought and adds variation, embellishment and adornment to literary works.

In figurative language we use words in such a way that they differ somewhat from ordinary every-day speech and convey meanings in a more vivid and impressive manner. Figures, like metonymy make speech more effective, they beautify and emphasise it in rhetoric which is the art of speaking and writing effectively. Figures of speech such as metonymy use word association to convey emotion and mood often in a non-literal sense.

Figures of speech such as metonymy adds adornment, beautifies, colors, elegant variation, embellishment, embroidery, emphasis, exaggeration, exclamation, flourish, floweriness, irony, lushness and luxuriance to the English language.

Poems with metonymy examples can be found as follows:

– "He writes a fine hand" meaning good handwriting.

– "The pen is mightier than the sword," meaning literary power is superior to military force.

– "The House was called to order," meaning the members in the House.

– "We have always remained loyal to the crown."

– "He is a man of the cloth."

– "By the sweat of thy brow thou shalt eat thy bread."

Exclamation

Exclamation (from the Latin *ex*, out, and *clamare*, to cry), is a figure by which the speaker instead of stating a fact, simply utters an expression of surprise or emotion. For instance when he hears some harrowing tale of woe or misfortune instead of saying,–"It is a sad story" he exclaims "What a sad story!"

Exclamation may be defined as the vocal expression of feeling, though it is also applied to written forms which are intended to express emotion. Thus in describing a towering mountain we can write "Heavens, what a piece of Nature's handiwork! how majestic! how sublime! how awe-inspiring in its colossal impressiveness!" This figure rather belongs to poetry and animated oratory than to the cold prose of everyday conversation and writing.

Apostrophe

Apostrophe is an exclamatory rhetorical figure of speech is an exclamatory rhetorical figure of speech, when a talker or writer breaks off and directs speech to an imaginary person or abstract quality or idea. In dramatic works and poetry written in or translated into English, such a figure of speech is often introduced by the exclamation "O".

It is related to personification, although in apostrophe, objects or abstractions are implied to have certain human qualities (such as understanding) by the very fact that the speaker is addressing them as he would a person in his presence.

Apostrophe is often used to convey extreme emotion, as in Claudius's impassioned speech in Hamlet.

Examples:

– "Where, O death, thy sting? where, O death, thy victory?" 1 Corinthians 15:55, traditionally attributed to Saint Paul.

- "O Romeo, Romeo! wherefore art thou Romeo?" Shakespeare, *Romeo and Juliet*, Act II, Scene 2
- "O, pardon me, thou bleeding piece of earth, / That I am meek and gentle with these butchers! / Thou art the ruins of the noblest man / That ever lived in the tide of times." Shakespeare, *Julius Caesar*, Act 3, Scene 1
- "To what green altar, O mysterious priest, / Lead'st thou that heifer lowing at the skies, / And all her silken flanks with garlands drest?" John Keats, "Ode on a Grecian Urn"
- "O eloquent, just, and mighty Death!" Sir Walter Raleigh, *A Historie of the World*
- "Roll on thou dark and deep blue ocean." Lord Byron, "Childe Harold's Pilgrimage"
- "Science! True daughter of Old Time thou art!" Edgar Allan Poe, "To Science"
- Common usage as an opposition speaker at a political convention: "And I say to you, Mr. President, we do not want our children to grow up in a world where...(etc.)"
- *O Captain! My Captain!*, title of Walt Whitman's poem

Vision

Vision is another figure of speech, which is proper only in animated and warm composition. It is produced when, instead of relating something that is past, we use the present tense, and describe it as actually passing before our eyes. Thus Cicero, in his fourth oration against Catiline: "I seem to myself to behold this city, the ornament of the earth, and the capital of all nations, suddenly involved in one conflagration. I see before me the slaughtered heaps of citizens, lying unburied in the midst of their ruined country. The furious countenance of Cethegus rises to my view, while with a savage joy, he is triumphing in your miseries." This manner of description supposes a sort of enthusiasm, which carries the person who describes, in some measure out of himself; and, when well executed, must needs, by the force of sympathy, impress the reader or hearer very strongly.

Antithesis

The next figure in order, is *Antithesis*. Comparison is founded on the resemblance; antithesis, on the contrast or opposition of two objects. Contrast has always the effect, to make each of the contrasted objects appear in the stronger light. White, for instance, never appears so bright as when it is opposed to black; and when both are viewed together. An author, in his defence of a friend against the charge of murder, expresses himself thus: "Can you believe that the person whom he scrupled to slay, when he might have done so with full justice, in a convenient place, at a proper time, with secure impunity; he made no scruple to murder against justice, in an unfavourable place, at an unseasonable time, and at the risk of capital condemnation?" The following examples further illustrate this figure.

- Tho' deep, yet clear; tho' gentle, yet not dull;
  Strong, without rage; without o'erflowing, full.
- "If you wish to enrich a person, study not to increase his stores, but to diminish his desires."
- "If you regulate your desires according to the standard of nature, you will never be poor; if according to the standard of opinion, you will never be rich."

Maxims

A *maxim*, or moral saying, very properly receives the form of the two last examples; both because it is supposed to be the fruit of meditation, and because it is designed to be engraven on the memory, which recalls it more easily by the help of such contrasted expressions. But where such sentences frequently succeed each other; where this becomes an author's favourite and prevailing manner of expressing himself, his style appears too much studied and laboured; it gives us the impression of an author attending more to his manner of saying things, than to the things themselves.

Interrogation

The unfigured, literal use of interrogation, is to ask a question: but when men are strongly moved, whatever they would affirm or deny, with great earnestness, they naturally put in the form of a question, expressing thereby the strongest confidence of the truth of their own sentiment, and appealing to their hearers for the impossibility of the contrary....

Interrogation gives life and spirit to discourse. We see this in the animated, introductory speech of Cicero against Catiline: "How long will you, Catiline, abuse our patience? Do you not perceive that your designs are discovered?" He might indeed have said; "You abuse our patience a long while. You must be sensible, that your designs are discovered." But it is easy to perceive, how much this latter mode of expression, falls short of the force and vehemence of the former.

Irony

Irony is expressing ourselves in a manner contrary to our thoughts, not with a view to deceive, but to add force to our observations. Persons may be reproved for their negligence, by saying; "You have taken great care indeed." Cicero says of the person against whom he was pleading; "We have great reason to believe that the modest man would not ask him for his debt, when he pursues his life."

Ironical exhortation is a very agreeable kind of figure; which, after having set the inconveniences of a thing, in the clearest light, concludes with a feigned encouragement to pursue it. Such is that of Horace, when, having beautifully described the noise and tumults of Rome, he adds ironically; "Go now, and study tuneful verse at Rome."

The subjects of Irony are vices and follies of all kinds: and this mode of exposing them, is often more effectual than serious reasoning. The gravest persons have not declined the use of this figure, on proper occasions. The wise and virtuous Socrates made great use of it, in his endeavours to discountenance vicious and foolish practices....

Exclamations and Irony are sometimes united: as in Cicero's oration for Balbus, where he derides his accuser, by saying; " O excellent interpreter of the law! master of antiquity! corrector and amender of our constitution."

Amplification and Climax

The last figure of speech that we shall mention, is what writers call *Amplification* or *Climax*. It consists in heightening all the circumstances of an object or action, which we desire to place in a strong light. Cicero gives a lively instance of this figure, when he says; "It is a crime to put a Roman citizen in bondst; it is the height of guilt to scourge him; little less than parricide to put him to death: what name then shall I give to the act of crucifying him?"...

Let us look at an example of a beautiful climax, taken from the charge of a judge to the jury, in the case of a woman accused of murdering her own child. "Gentlemen, if one man had any how slain another; if an adversary had killed his opposer, or a woman occasioned the death of her enemy; even these criminals would have been capitally punished by the Cornelian law; but if this guiltless infant, that could make no enemy, had been murdered by its own nurse, what punishment would not then the mother have demanded? With what cries and exclamations would she have stunned your ears! What shall we say then, when a woman, guilty of homicide, a mother, of the murder of her innocent child, hath comprised all those misdeeds in one single crime? a crime, in its own nature, detestable; in a woman prodigious; in a mother, incredible; and perpetrated against one whose age called for compassion, whose near relation claimed affection, and whose innocence deserved the highest favour."

Rules of Using Figures of Speech

We have now finished what was proposed, concerning Perspicuity in single words and phrases, and the accurate construction of sentences. The former has been considered under the heads of Purity, Propriety, and Precision; and the latter, under those of Clearness, Unity, Strength, and the proper use of Figurative Language. Though many of those attentions which have been recommended, may appear minute, yet their effect upon writing and style, is much greater than might, at first, be imagined. A sentiment which is expressed in accurate language, and in a period, clearly, neatly, and well arranged, always makes a stronger impression on the mind, than one that is expressed inaccurately, or in a feeble or embarrassed manner. Every one feels this upon a comparison: and if the effect be sensible in one sentence, how much more in a whole discourse, or composition that is made up of such sentences?

The fundamental rule for writing with accuracy, and into which all others might be resolved, undoubtedly is, *to communicate, in correct language, and in the clearest and most natural order, the ideas which we mean to transfuse into the minds of others*. Such a selection and arrangement of words, as do most justice to the sense, and express it to most advantage, make an agreeable and strong impression. To these points have tended all the rules which have been given.

Advantages

The principal advantages of figures of speech, are the two following:

First, They enrich language and render it more copious. By their means, words and phrases are multiplied, for expressing all sorts of ideas; for describing even the minutest differences; the nicest shades and colours of thought; which no language could possibly do by proper words alone, without assistance from Tropes.

Secondly, They frequently give us a much clearer and more striking view of the principal object, than we could have, if it were expressed in simple terms, and divested of its accessory idea. By a well-chosen figure, even conviction is assisted, and the impression of a truth upon the mind, made more lively and forcible than it would otherwise be. We perceive this in the following illustration of Young: " When we dip too deep in pleasure, we always stir a sediment that renders it impure and noxious"; and in this instance: " A heart boiling with violent passions, will always send up infatuating fumes to the head." An image that presents so much congruity between a moral and a sensible idea, serves, like an argument from analogy, to enforce what the author asserts, and to induce belief.

5

Word Choice

Writing is a series of choices. As you work on a paper, you choose your topic, your approach, your sources, and your thesis; when it's time to write, you have to choose the words you will use to express your ideas and decide how you will arrange those words into sentences and paragraphs. As you revise your draft, you make more choices. You might ask yourself, "Is this really what I mean?" or "Will readers understand this?" or "Does this sound good?" Finding words that capture your meaning and convey that meaning to your readers is challenging. When your instructors write things like "awkward," "vague," or "wordy" on your draft, they are letting you know that they want you to work on word choice. This handout will explain some common issues related to word choice and give you strategies for choosing the best words as you revise your drafts.

Keep in mind that it can sometimes take more time to "save" words from your original sentence than to write a brand new sentence to convey the same meaning or idea. Don't be too attached to what you've already written; if you are willing to start a sentence fresh, you may be able to choose words with greater clarity.

Words from Different Sources

The English language is the tongue now current in

England and her colonies throughout the world and also throughout the greater part of the United States of America. It sprang from the German tongue spoken by the Teutons, who came over to Britain after the conquest of that country by the Romans. These Teutons comprised Angles, Saxons, Jutes and several other tribes from the northern part of Germany. They spoke different dialects, but these became blended in the new country, and the composite tongue came to be known as the Anglo-Saxon which has been the main basis for the language as at present constituted and is still the prevailing element. Therefore those who are trying to do away with some of the purely Anglo-Saxon words, on the ground that they are not refined enough to express their aesthetic ideas, are undermining main props which are necessary for the support of some important parts in the edifice of the language.

The Anglo-Saxon element supplies the essential parts of speech, the article, pronoun of all kinds, the preposition, the auxiliary verbs, the conjunctions, and the little particles which bind words into sentences and form the joints, sinews and ligaments of the language. It furnishes the most indispensable words of the vocabulary. Nowhere is the beauty of Anglo-Saxon better illustrated than in the Lord's Prayer. Fifty-four words are pure Saxon and the remaining ones could easily be replaced by Saxon words. The gospel of St. John is another illustration of the almost exclusive use of Anglo-Saxon words. Shakespeare, at his best, is Anglo-Saxon. Here is a quotation from the Merchant of Venice, and of the fifty-five words fifty-two are Anglo-Saxon, the remaining three French:

All that glitters is not gold—
Often have you heard that told;
Many a man his life hath sold,
But my outside to behold.

Guilded tombs do worms infold.
Had you been as wise as bold,
Young in limbs, in judgment old,
Your answer had not been inscrolled—
Fare you well, your suit is cold.

The lines put into the mouth of Hamlet's father in fierce intenseness, second only to Dante's inscription on the gate of hell, have one hundred and eight Anglo-Saxon and but fifteen Latin words.

The second constituent element of present English is Latin which comprises those words derived directly from the old Roman and those which came indirectly through the French. The former were introduced by the Roman Christians, who came to England at the close of the sixth century under Augustine, and relate chiefly to ecclesiastical affairs, such as saint from *sanctus*, religion from *religio*, chalice from *calix*, mass from *missa*, etc. Some of them had origin in Greek, as priest from presbyter, which in turn was a direct derivative from the Greek *presbuteros*, also deacon from the Greek *diakonos*.

The largest class of Latin words are those which came through the Norman-French, or Romance. The Normans had adopted, with the Christian religion, the language, laws and arts of the Romanised Gauls and Romanised Franks, and after a residence of more than a century in France they successfully invaded England in 1066 under William the Conqueror and a new era began. The French Latinisms can be distinguished by the spelling. Thus Saviour comes from the Latin Salvator through the French Sauveur; judgment from the Latin judiclum through the French jugement; people, from the Latin *populus*, through the French *peuple*, etc.

For a long time the Saxon and Norman tongues refused to coalesce and were like two distinct currents flowing in different directions. Norman was spoken by the lords and barons in their feudal castles, in parliament and in the courts of justice. Saxon by the people in their rural homes, fields and workshops. For more than three hundred years the streams flowed apart, but finally they blended, taking in the Celtic and Danish elements, and as a result came the present English language with its simple system of grammatical inflection and its rich vocabulary.

The father of English prose is generally regarded as Wycliffe, who translated the Bible in 1380, while the paternal laurels in the secular poetical field are twined around the brows of Chaucer.

Besides the Germanic and Romanic, which constitute the greater part of the English language, many other tongues have furnished their quota. Of these the Celtic is perhaps the oldest. The Britons at Caesar's invasion, were a part of the Celtic family. The Celtic idiom is still spoken in two dialects, the Welsh in Wales, and the Gaelic in Ireland and the Highlands of Scotland. The Celtic words in English, are comparatively few; cart, dock, wire, rail, rug, cradle, babe, grown, griddle, lad, lass, are some in most common use.

The Danish element dates from the piratical invasions of the ninth and tenth centuries. It includes anger, awe, baffle, bang, bark, bawl, blunder, boulder, box, club, crash, dairy, dazzle, fellow, gable, gain, ill, jam, kidnap, kill, kidney, kneel, limber, litter, log, lull, lump, mast, mistake, nag, nasty, niggard, horse, plough, rug, rump, sale, scald, shriek, skin, skull, sledge, sleigh, tackle, tangle, tipple, trust, viking, window, wing, etc.

From the Hebrew we have a large number of proper names from Adam and Eve down to John and Mary and such words as Messiah, rabbi, hallelujah, cherub, seraph, hosanna, manna, satan, Sabbath, etc.

Many technical terms and names of branches of learning come from the Greek. In fact, nearly all the terms of learning and art, from the alphabet to the highest peaks of metaphysics and theology, come directly from the Greek—philosophy, logic, anthropology, psychology, aesthetics, grammar, rhetoric, history, philology, mathematics, arithmetic, astronomy, anatomy, geography, stenography, physiology, architecture, and hundreds more in similar domains; the subdivisions and ramifications of theology as exegesis, hermeneutics, apologetics, polemics, dogmatics, ethics, homiletics, etc., are all Greek.

The Dutch have given us some modern sea terms, as sloop, schooner, yacht and also a number of others as boom, bush, boor, brandy, duck, reef, skate, wagon. The Dutch of Manhattan island gave us boss, the name for employer or overseer, also *cold slaa* (cut cabbage and vinegar), and a number of geographical terms.

Many of our most pleasing euphonic words, especially in the realm of music, have been given to us directly from the Italian. Of these are piano, violin, orchestra, canto, allegro, piazza, gazette, umbrella, gondola, bandit, etc.

Spanish has furnished us with alligator, alpaca, bigot, cannibal, cargo, filibuster, freebooter, guano, hurricane, mosquito, negro, stampede, potato, tobacco, tomato, tariff, etc.

From Arabic we have several mathematical, astronomical, medical and chemical terms as alcohol, alcove, alembic, algebra, alkali, almanac, assassin, azure, cipher, elixir, harem, hegira, sofa, talisman, zenith and zero.

Bazaar, dervish, lilac, pagoda, caravan, scarlet, shawl, tartar, tiara and peach have come to us from the Persian.

Turban, tulip, divan and firman are Turkish.

Drosky, knout, rouble, steppe, ukase are Russian.

The Indians have helped english considerably and the words they have given to english are extremely euphonic as exemplified in the names of many rivers and States, as Mississippi, Missouri, Minnehaha, Susqu-ehanna, Monongahela, Niagara, Ohio, Massachusetts, Connecticut, Iowa, Nebraska, Dakota, etc. In addition to these proper names we have from the Indians wigwam, squaw, hammock, tomahawk, canoe, mocassin, hominy, etc.

There are many hybrid words in English, that is, words, springing from two or more different languages. In fact, English has drawn from all sources, and it is daily adding to its already large family, and not alone is it adding to itself, but it is spreading all over the world and promises to take in the entire human family beneath its folds were long. It is the opinion of many that English, in a short time, will become the universal language. It is now being taught as a branch of the higher education in the best colleges and universities of Europe and in all commercial cities in every land throughout the world.

In Asia it follows the British sway and the highways of commerce through the vast empire of East India with its two hundred and fifty millions of heathen and Mohammedan inhabitants. It is largely used in the seaports of Japan and China, and the number of natives of these countries who are learning it is increasing every day. It is firmly established in South Africa, Liberia, Sierra Leone, and in many of the islands of the Indian and South Seas. It is the language of Australia, New Zealand, Tasmania, and Christian missionaries are introducing it into all the islands of Polynesia.

It may be said to be the living commercial language of the North American continent, from Baffin's Bay to the

Gulf of Mexico, and from the Atlantic to the Pacific, and it is spoken largely in many of the republics of South America. It is not limited by parallels of latitude, or meridians of longitude. The two great English-speaking countries, England and the United States, are disseminating it north, south, east and west over the entire world.

Difficulties with Word Choice

You write a paper that makes perfect sense to you, but it comes back with "awkward" scribbled throughout the margins. Why, you wonder, are instructors so fond of terms like "awkward"? Most instructors use terms like this to draw your attention to sentences they had trouble understanding and to encourage you to rewrite those sentences more clearly.

Difficulties with word choice aren't the only cause of awkwardness, vagueness, or other problems with clarity. Sometimes a sentence is hard to follow because there is a grammatical problem with it or because of the syntax (the way the words and phrases are put together). Here's an example: "Having finished with studying, the pizza was quickly eaten." This sentence isn't hard to understand because of the words I chose—everybody knows what studying, pizza, and eating are. The problem here is that readers will naturally assume that first bit of the sentence "(Having finished with studying") goes with the next noun that follows it—which, in this case, is "the pizza"! It doesn't make a lot of sense to imply that the pizza was studying. What I was actually trying to express was something more like this: "Having finished with studying, the students quickly ate the pizza." If you have a sentence that has been marked "awkard," "vague," or "unclear," try to think about it from a reader's point of view—see if you can tell where it changes direction or leaves out important information.

Sometimes, though, problems with clarity are a matter of word choice. See if you recognise any of these issues:

1. *Misused words—The word doesn't actually mean what the writer thinks it does.*

   Example: Cree Indians were a monotonous culture until French and British settlers arrived.

   Revision: Cree Indians were a homogenous culture.

2. *Words with unwanted connotations or meanings.*

   Example: I sprayed the ants in their private places.

   Revision: I sprayed the ants in their hiding places.

3. *Using a pronoun when readers can't tell whom/what it refers to.*

   Example: My cousin Sachin hugged my brother Sourav, even though he didn't like him very much.

   Revision: My cousin Sachin hugged my brother Sourav, even though Sachin doesn't like Sourav very much.

4. *Jargon or technical terms that make readers work unnecessarily hard. Maybe you need to use some of these words because they are important terms in your field, but don't throw them in just to "sound smart."*

   Example: The dialectical interface between neo-Platonists and anti-disestablishment Catholics offers an algorithm for deontological thought.

   Revision: The dialogue between neo-Platonists and certain Catholic thinkers is a model for deontological thought.

5. *Loaded language*. Sometimes we as writers know what we mean by a certain word, but we haven't ever spelled that out for readers. We rely too heavily on that word, perhaps repeating it often, without clarifying what we are talking about.

Example: Society teaches young girls that beauty is their most important quality. In order to prevent eating disorders and other health problems, we must change society.

Revision: Contemporary Indian media, like magazines and movies, teach young girls that beauty is their most important quality. In order to prevent eating disorders and other health problems, we must change the images and role models girls are offered.

Wordiness

Sometimes the problem isn't choosing exactly the right word to express an idea—it's being "wordy," or using words that your reader may regard as "extra" or inefficient. Take a look at the following list for some examples. On the left are some phrases that use three, four, or more words where fewer will do; on the right are some shorter substitutes:

I came to the realization that	I realized that
She is of the opinion that	She thinks that
Concerning the matter of	About
During the course of	During
In the event that	If
In the process of	During, while
Regardless of the fact that	Although
Due to the fact that	Because
In all cases	Always
At that point in time	Then
Prior to	Before

Keep an eye out for wordy constructions in your writing and see if you can replace them with more concise words or phrases.

Cliches

In academic writing, it is a good idea to limit your use of cliches. Cliches are catchy little phrases so frequently used that they have become trite, corny, or annoying. They are problematic because their overuse has diminished their impact and because they require several words where just one would do.

The main way to avoid clichés is first to recognise them and then to create shorter, fresher equivalents. Ask yourself if there is one word that means the same thing as the cliché. If there isn't, can you use two or three words to state the idea your own way? Below you will see five common clichés, with some alternatives to their right. As a challenge, see how many alternatives you can create for the final two examples.

Agree to disagree	Disagree
Dead as a doornail	Dead
Last but not least	Last
Pushing the envelope	Approaching the limit
Up in the air	Unknown/undecided

Writing for an Academic Audience

When you choose words to express your ideas, you have to think not only about what makes sense and sounds best to you, but what will make sense and sound best to your readers. Thinking about your audience and their expectations will help you make decisions about word choice.

Some writers think that academic audiences expect them to "sound smart" by using big or technical words. But the most important goal of academic writing is not to sound smart—it is to communicate an argument or information clearly and convincingly. It is true that academic writing has a certain style of its own and that you, as a student, are beginning to learn to read and write in that style. You may find yourself using words and grammatical constructions that you didn't use in your high school writing. The danger is that if you consciously set out to "sound smart" and use words or structures that are very unfamiliar to you, you may produce sentences that your readers can't understand.

When writing for your professors, think simplicity. Using simple words does not indicate simple thoughts. In an academic argument paper, what makes the thesis and argument sophisticated are the connections presented in simple, clear language.

Keep in mind, though, that simple and clear doesn't necessarily mean casual. Most instructors will not be pleased if your paper looks like an instant message or an email to a friend. It's usually best to avoid slang and colloquialisms.

Selecting Words

Words of "learned length and thundering sound" should be avoided on all possible occasions. They proclaim shallowness of intellect and vanity of mind. The great purists, the masters of diction, the exemplars of style, used short, simple words that all could understand; words about which there could be no ambiguity as to meaning. It must be remembered that by our words we teach others; therefore, a very great responsibility rests upon us in regard to the use of a right language. We must take care that we think and speak in a way so clear that there may be no misapprehension or danger of conveying wrong impressions by vague and misty ideas enunciated in terms which are liable to be misunderstood by those whom we address.

Words give a body or form to our ideas, without which they are apt to be so foggy that we do not see where they are weak or false. We must make the endeavour to employ such words as will put the idea we have in our own mind into the mind of another. This is the greatest art in the world–to clothe our ideas in words clear and comprehensive to the intelligence of others. It is the art which the teacher, the minister, the lawyer, the orator, the business man, must master if they would command success in their various fields of endeavour. It is very hard to convey an idea to, and impress it on, another when he has but a faint conception of the language in which the idea is expressed; but it is impossible to convey it at all when the words in which it is clothed are unintelligible to the listener.

If we address an audience of ordinary men and women in the English language, but use such words as they cannot comprehend, we might as well speak to them in Coptic or Chinese, for they will derive no benefit from our address, inasmuch as the ideas we wish to convey are expressed in words which communicate no intelligent meaning to their minds.

Long words, learned words, words directly derived from other languages are only understood by those who have had the advantages of an extended education. All have not had such advantages. The great majority in this grand and glorious country of ours have to hustle for a living from an early age. Though education is free, and compulsory also, very many never get further than the "Three R's." These are the men with whom we have to deal most in the arena of life, the men with the horny palms and the iron muscles, the men who build our houses, construct our railroads, drive our street cars and trains, till our fields, harvest our crops–in a word, the men who form the foundation of all society, the men on whom the world depends to make its wheels go round.

The language of the colleges and universities is not for them and they can get along very well without it; they have no need for it at all in their respective callings. The plain, simple words of everyday life, to which the common people have been used around their own firesides from childhood, are the words we must use in our dealings with them.

Such words are understood by them and understood by the learned as well; why then not use them universally and all the time? Why make a one-sided affair of language by using words which only one class of the people, the so-called learned class, can understand? Would it not be better to use, on all occasions, language which the both classes can understand? If we take the trouble to investigate we shall find that the men who exerted the greatest sway over the masses and the multitude as orators, lawyers, preachers and in other public capacities, were men who used very simple language.

Daniel Webster was among the greatest orators this country has produced. He touched the hearts of senates and assemblages, of men and women with the burning eloquence of his words. He never used a long word when he could convey the same, or nearly the same, meaning with a short one. When he made a speech he always told those who put it in form for the press to strike out every long word. Study his speeches, go over all he ever said or wrote, and you will find that his language was always made up of short, clear, strong terms, although at times, for the sake of sound and oratorical effect, he was compelled to use a rather long word, but it was always against his inclination to do so, and where was the man who could paint, with words, as Webster painted! He could picture things in a way so clear that those who heard him felt that they had seen that of which he spoke.

Abraham Lincoln was another who stirred the souls of men, yet he was not an orator, not a scholar; he did not write M.A. or Ph.D. after his name, or any other college degree, for he had none. He graduated from the University of Hard Knocks, and he never forgot this severe *Alma Mater* when he became President of the United States. He was just as plain, I just as humble, as in the days when he split rails or plied a boat on the Sangamon. He did not use big words, but he used the words of the people, and in such a way as to make them beautiful. His Gettysburg address is an English classic, one of the great masterpieces of the language.

From the mere fact that a word is short it does not follow that it is always clear, but it is true that nearly all clear words are short, and that most of the long words, especially those which we get from other languages, are misunderstood to a great extent by the ordinary rank and file of the people. Indeed, it is to be doubted if some of the "scholars" using them, fully understand their import on occasions. A great many such words admit of several interpretations. A word has to be in use a great deal before people get thoroughly familiar with its meaning. Long words, not alone obscure thought and make the ideas hazy, but at times they tend to mix up things in such a way that positively harmful results follow from their use.

For instance, crime can be so covered with the folds of long words as to give it a different appearance. Even the hideousness of sin can be cloaked with such words until its outlines look like a thing of beauty. When a bank cashier makes off with a hundred thousand dollars we politely term his crime defalcation instead of plain theft, and instead of calling himself a thief we grandiosely allude to him as a defaulter.

When we see a wealthy man staggering along a fashionable thoroughfare under the influence of alcohol, waving his arms in the air and shouting boisterously, we smile and say, poor gentleman, he is somewhat exhilarated; or at worst we say, he is slightly inebriated; but when we see a poor man who has fallen from grace by putting an "enemy into his mouth to steal away his brain" we express our indignation in the simple language of the words: "Look at the wretch; he is dead drunk."

When we find a person in downright lying we cover the falsehood with the finely-spun cloak of the word prevarication. Shakespeare says, "a rose by any other name would smell as sweet," and by a similar sequence, a lie, no matter by what name you may call it, is always a lie and should be condemned; then why not simply call it a lie? Mean what you say and say what you mean; call a spade a spade, it is the best term you can apply to the implement.

When you try to use short words and shun long ones in a little while you will find that you can do so with ease. A farmer was showing a horse to a city-bred gentleman. The animal was led into a paddock in which an old sow-pig was rooting. "What a fine quadruped!" exclaimed the city man.

"Which of the two do you mean, the pig or the horse?" queried the farmer, "for, in my opinion, both of them are fine quadrupeds."

Of course the visitor meant the horse, so it would have been much better had he called the animal by its simple; ordinary name–, there would have been no room for ambiguity in his remark. He profited, however, by the incident, and never called a horse a quadruped again.

Most of the small words, the simple words, the beautiful words which express so much within small bounds belong to the pure Anglo-Saxon element of our language. This element has given names to the heavenly bodies, the sun, moon and stars; to three out of the four elements, earth, fire and water; three out of the four seasons, spring, summer and winter. Its simple words are applied to all the natural divisions of time, except one, as day, night, morning, evening, twilight, noon, mid-day, midnight, sunrise and sunset. The names of light, heat, cold, frost, rain, snow, hail, sleet, thunder, lightning, as well as almost all those objects which form the component parts of the beautiful, as expressed in external scenery, such as sea and land, hill and dale, wood and stream, etc., are Anglo-Saxon. To this same language we are indebted for those words which express the earliest and dearest connections, and the strongest and most powerful feelings of Nature, and which, as a consequence, are interwoven with the fondest and most hallowed associations. Of such words are father, mother, husband, wife, brother, sister, son, daughter, child, home, kindred, friend, hearth, roof and fireside.

The chief emotions of which we are susceptible are expressed in the same language–love, hope, fear, sorrow, shame, and also the outward signs by which these emotions are indicated, as tear, smile, laugh, blush, weep, sigh, groan. Nearly all our national proverbs are Anglo-Saxon. Almost all the terms and phrases by which we most energetically express anger, contempt and indignation are of the same origin.

What are known as the smart set and so-called polite society, are relegating a great many of our old Anglo-Saxon words into the shade, faithful friends who served their ancestors well. These self-appointed arbiters of diction regard some of the Anglo-Saxon words as too coarse, too plebeian for their aesthetic tastes and refined ears, so they are eliminating them from their vocabulary and replacing them with mongrels of foreign birth and hybrids of unknown origin. For the ordinary people, however, the man in the street or in the field, the woman in the kitchen or in the factory, they are still tried and true and, like old friends, should be cherished and preferred to all strangers, no matter from what source the latter may spring.

Repetition *vs.* Redundancy

These two phenomena are not necessarily the same. Repetition can be a good thing. Sometimes we have to use our key terms several times within a paper, especially in topic sentences. Sometimes there is simply no substitute for the key terms, and selecting a weaker term as a synonym can do more harm than good. Repeating key terms emphasises important points and signals to the reader that the argument is still being supported. This kind of repetition can give your paper cohesion and is done by conscious choice.

In contrast, if you find yourself frustrated, tiredly repeating the same nouns, verbs, or adjectives, or making the same point over and over, you are probably being redundant. In this case, you are swimming aimlessly around the same points because you have not decided what your argument really is or because you are truly fatigued and clarity escapes you.

Building Clear Statements

Writing clear sentences is important throughout our writing. For the purposes of this handout, let's focus on the thesis statement—one of the most important sentences in academic argument papers. You can apply these ideas to other sentences in your papers.

A common problem with writing good thesis statements is finding the words that best capture both the important elements and the significance of the essay's argument. It is not always easy to condense several paragraphs or several pages into concise key terms that, when combined in one sentence, can effectively describe the argument.

However, taking the time to find the right words offers writers a significant edge. Concise and appropriate terms will help both the writer and the reader keep track of what the essay will show and how it will show it. Graders, in particular, like to see clearly stated thesis statements.

Example: You've been assigned to write an essay that contrasts the river and shore scenes in Mark Twain's *Huckleberry Finn*. You work on it for several days, producing three versions of your thesis:

- *Version 1*: There are many important river and shore scenes in *Huckleberry Finn*.
- *Version 2*: The contrasting river and shore scenes in *Huckleberry Finn* suggest a return to nature.
- *Version 3*: Through its contrasting river and shore scenes, *Twain's Huckleberry Finn* suggests that to find the true expression of American democratic ideals, one must leave "civilised" society and go back to nature.

Let's consider the word choice issues in these statements. In Version 1, the word "important"—like "interesting"—is both overused and vague; it suggests that the author has an opinion but gives very little indication about the framework of that opinion. As a result, your reader knows only that you're going to talk about river and shore scenes, but not what you're going to say. Version 2 is an improvement: the words "return to nature" give your reader a better idea where the paper is headed. On the other hand, she still does not know how this return to nature is crucial to your understanding of the novel.

Finally, you come up with Version 3, which is a stronger thesis because it offers a sophisticated argument and the key terms used to make this argument are clear. At least three key terms or concepts are evident: the contrast between river and shore scenes, a return to nature, and American democratic ideals.

By itself, a key term is merely a topic—an element of the argument but not the argument itself. The argument, then, becomes clear to the reader through the way in which you combine key terms.

Strategies for Successful Word Choice

1. Be careful when using words you are unfamiliar with. Look at how they are used in context and check their dictionary definitions.
2. Be careful when using the thesaurus. Each word listed as a synonym for the word you're looking up may have its own unique connotations or shades of meaning. Use a dictionary to be sure the synonym you are considering really fits what you are trying to say.
3. Don't try to impress your reader or sound unduly authoritative. For example, which sentence is clearer to you: "a" or "b"?
4. Under the present conditions of our society, marriage practices generally demonstrate a high degree of homogeneity.

5 In our culture, people tend to marry others who are like themselves.

6. Before you revise for accurate and strong adjectives, make sure you are first using accurate and strong nouns and verbs. For example, if you were revising the sentence "This is a good book that tells about the Gulf War," think about whether "book" and "tells" are as strong as they could be before you worry about "good."

7. Try the slash/option technique, which is like brainstorming as you write. When you get stuck, write out two or more choices for a questionable word or a confusing sentence, e.g., "questionable/inaccurate/vague/inappropriate." Pick the word that best indicates your meaning or combine different terms to say what you mean.

8. Look for repetition. When you find it, decide if it is "good" repetition (using key terms that are crucial and helpful to meaning) or "bad" repetition (redundancy or laziness in reusing words).

9. Write your thesis in five different ways. Make five different versions of your thesis sentence. Compose five sentences that express your argument. Try to come up with four alternatives to the thesis sentence you've already written. Find five possible ways to communicate your argument in one sentence to your reader.

10. Whenever we write a sentence we make choices. Some are less obvious than others, so that it can often feel like we've written the sentence the only way we know how. By writing out five different versions of your thesis, you can begin to see your range of choices. The final version may be a combination of phrasings and words from all five versions, or the one version that says it best. By

literally spelling out some possibilities for yourself, you will be able to make better decisions.

11. Read your paper out loud and at... a... slow... pace. You can do this alone or with a friend, roommate, TA, etc. When read out loud, your written words should make sense to both you and other listeners. If a sentence seems confusing, rewrite it to make the meaning clear.
12. Instead of reading the paper itself, put it down and just talk through your argument as concisely as you can. If your listener quickly and easily comprehends your essay's main point and significance, you should then make sure that your written words are as clear as your oral presentation was. If, on the other hand, your listener keeps asking for clarification, you will need to work on finding the right terms for your essay. If you do this in exchange with a friend or classmate, rest assured that whether you are the talker or the listener, your articulation skills will develop.
13. Have someone not familiar with the issue read the paper and point out words or sentences he/she finds confusing. Do not brush off this reader's confusion by assuming he or she simply doesn't know enough about the topic. Instead, rewrite the sentences so that your "outsider" reader can follow along at all times.

6

Punctuation and Capitalisation Rules

The rules for using punctuation would never hold up in court. These rules, in fact, are conventions that have changed over the centuries. They vary across national boundaries and even from one writer to the next.

Until the 18th century, punctuation was primarily related to spoken delivery (elocution), and the marks were interpreted as pauses that could be counted out. For example, in *An Essay on Elocution,* John Mason suggested this sequence of pauses: "A Comma stops the Voice while we may privately tell one, a semi-colon two; a colon three; and a Period four." This declamatory basis for punctuation gradually gave way to the syntactic approach used today.

Understanding the principles behind the common marks of punctuation should strengthen your understanding of grammar and help you to use the marks consistently in your own writing. Punctuation has the primary responsibility of contributing to the plainness of one's meaning. It has the secondary responsibility of being as invisible as possible, of not calling attention to itself.

The chief end of punctuation is to mark the grammatical connection and the dependence of the parts of a composition, but not the actual pauses made in speaking. Very often the points used to denote the delivery of a passage differ from those used when the passage is written. Nevertheless, several of the punctuation marks serve to bring out the rhetorical force of expression.

The principal marks of punctuation are:

1. The Comma [,]
2. The Semicolon [;]
3. The Colon [:]
4. The Period [.]
5. The Interrogation [?]
6. The Exclamation [!]
7. The Dash [—]
8. The Parenthesis [()]
9. The Quotation [" "]

Of the above, the first four may be styled the grammatical points, and the remaining five, the rhetorical points.

The Comma

The most popular mark of punctuation, the comma (,) is also the least law-abiding. In Greek, the *komma* was a "piece cut off" from a line of verse—what in English today we'd call a phrase or a clause. Since the 16th century, comma has referred to the mark that sets off words, phrases, and clauses.

The aim of the comma is to show the slightest separation which calls for punctuation at all. It should be omitted whenever possible. It is used to mark the least divisions of a sentence.

1. *A series of words or phrases has its parts separated by commas:–* "Lying, trickery, chicanery, perjury, were

natural to him." "The brave, daring, faithful soldier died facing the foe." If the series is in pairs, commas separate the pairs: "Rich and poor, learned and unlearned, black and white, Christian and Jew, Mohammedan and Buddhist must pass through the same gate."

2. *A comma is used before a short quotation*: "It was Patrick Henry who said, 'Give me liberty or give me death.'"
3. *When the subject of the sentence is a clause or a long phrase, a comma is used after such subject:* "That he has no reverence for the God I love, proves his insincerity." "Simulated piety, with a black coat and a sanctimonious look, does not proclaim a Christian."
4. *An expression used parenthetically should be inclosed by commas:* "The old man, as a general rule, takes a morning walk."
5. *Words in apposition are set off by commas:* "Indira Gandhi, the Prime Minister, was assassinated."
6. *Relative clauses, if not restrictive, require commas:* "The book, which is the simplest, is often the most profound."
7. *In continued sentences each should be followed by a comma*: "Electricity lights our dwellings and streets, pulls cars, trains, drives the engines of our mills and factories."
8. *When a verb is omitted a comma takes its place:* "Nehru was a great statesman; Grant, a great leader."
9. *The subject of address is followed by a comma*: "Rahul, you are a good man."
10. *In numeration, commas are used to express periods of three figures*: "Mountains 25,000 feet high; 1,000,000 Rupees."

SEMICOLON

The semicolon (;) is a period on top of a comma—looks as if it can't make up its mind. There's good reason for that: It shows a separation of thought that isn't quite complete. Beginning writers often think of semicolons as unncecessary. Why use them, they ask, when a comma or period will serve as well? In fact, semicolons serve a vital grammatical function that other pieces of punctuation cannot: they join together or clarify ideas that are closely related. As such, they should not be confused with commas, periods, or colons.

The semicolon is a separating elements but used much less than the comma. It is more often used in more advanced extended sentences and adds a formal tone. Its name implies that it indicates a separation that is neither full (as indicated by the period), nor minute (as indicated by a comma). The semicolon denotes a half-way separation between elements close in meaning. Skilled writers know that they should not overuse the semicolon but merely use for "spicing up" the text's punctuation. Do not simply use the semicolon instead of a comma in order to make the text appear "fancy."

Semicolons have many uses, but they are often misused. Learning why and how semicolons are used will help improve anybody's writing skills. So what is that little comma with a dot above it anyway? Sure it's sometimes seen between two sentences, but what other ways can it be used? And when should it be used? The semicolon is always used as a connecting punctuation; it is used to connect sentences or a list of items that has punctuation within it.

The semicolon marks a slighter connection than the comma. It is generally confined to separating the parts of compound sentences. It is much used in contrasts:

1. *Semicolon between two Sentences*: "Ambedkar was great as a statesman; he was sublime as a man."
2. *The Semicolon is used between the parts of all compound sentences in which the grammatical subject of the second part is different from that of the first:* "The power of India relies upon the wisdom of her statesmen; the power of America upon the strength of her army and navy."
3. *The Semicolon is used before words and abbreviations which introduce particulars or specifications following after, such as, namely, as, e.g., viz., i.e., etc.*: "He had three defects; namely, carelessness, lack of concentration and obstinacy in his ideas." "An island is a portion of land entirely surrounded by water; as Cuba." "The names of cities should always commence with a capital letter; *e.g.*, New Delhi, Mumbai." "The boy was proficient in one branch; viz., Mathematics." "No man is perfect; *i.e.*, free from all blemish."

Colon

The colon (:), consisting of two equally sized dots centred on the same vertical line. There are two ways to think of the colon: as a strong internal punctuation mark that indicates a long pause, and as a friendly, outgoing punctuation mark that introduces parts of a sentence. A colon may introduce a list of items, a long quotation, or an elaborated version of a point made in the first part of the sentence.

1. *It is generally put at the end of a sentence introducing a long quotation:* "The cheers having subsided, Mr. Khan spoke as follows:"
2. *It is placed before an explanation or illustration of the subject under consideration*: "This is the meaning of the term:"

3. *A direct quotation formally introduced is generally preceded by a colon:* "The great orator made this funny remark:"
4. *The colon is often used in the title of books when the secondary or subtitle is in apposition to the leading one and when the conjunction or is omitted:* "Acoustics: the Science of Sound."
5. *It is used after the salutation in the beginning of letters:* "Sir: My dear Sir: Gentlemen: Dear Mr. Arun:" etc. In this connection a dash very often follows the colon.
6. It *is sometimes used to introduce details of a group of things already referred to in the mass:* "The boy's excuses for being late were: firstly, he did not know the time, secondly, he was sent on an errand, thirdly, he tripped on a rock and fell by the wayside."

PERIOD

The period or full stop (.) is the simplest punctuation mark. It is simply used to mark the end of a complete sentence that is neither interrogative nor exclamatory.

1. After every sentence conveying a complete meaning: "Birds fly." "Plants grow." "Man is mortal."
2. In abbreviations: after every abbreviated word: Rt. Rev. T. C. Kahali, D.D., L.L.D.
3. A period is used on the title pages of books after the name of the book, after the author's name, after the publisher's imprint: *American Trails*. By Theodore Roosevelt. New York. Scribner Company.

QUESTION MARK

The main function of a question mark (?) is to indicate a

question or query. It can also be used mid-sentence to mark a merely interrogative phrase, where it functions similarly to a comma. The question mark character is often used in place of missing or unknown data.

1. Every question admitting of an answer, even when it is not expected, should be followed by the mark of interrogation: "Who has not heard of Emporer Ashoka?"
2. When several questions have a common dependence they should be followed by one mark of interrogation at the end of the series: "Where now are the playthings and friends of my boyhood; the laughing boys; the winsome girls; the fond neighbours whom I loved?"
3. The mark is often used parenthetically to suggest doubt: "In 1893 (?) Gladstone became converted to Home Rule for Ireland."

EXCLAMATION

The exclamation mark (!) should be sparingly used, particularly in prose. Its chief use is to denote emotion of some kind.

1. It is generally employed with interjections or clauses used as interjections: "Alas! I am forsaken." "What a lovely landscape!"
2. Expressions of strong emotion call for the exclamation: "Charge, Chester, charge! On, Stanley, on!"
3. When the emotion is very strong double exclamation points may be used: "Assist him!! I would rather assist Devil!!"

DASH

The Dash (—) is generally confined to cases where there

is a sudden break from the general run of the passage. Of all the punctuation marks it is the most misused.

1. It is employed to denote sudden change in the construction or sentiment: "The Heroes of the Kargil War,–how we cherish them." "He was a fine fellow–in his own opinion."
2. When a word or expression is repeated for oratorical effect, a dash is used to introduce the repetition: "Shakespeare was the greatest of all poets–Shakespeare, the intellectual ocean whose waves washed the continents of all thought."
3. The Dash is used to indicate a conclusion without expressing it: "He is an excellent man but–"
4. It is used to indicate what is not expected or what is not the natural outcome of what has gone before: "He delved deep into the bowels of the earth and found instead of the hidden treasure–a button."
5. It is used to denote the omission of letters or figures: "J–n J–s" for John Jones; 1908-9 for 1908 and 1909; Matthew VII:5-8 for Matthew VII:5, 6, 7, and 8.
6. When an ellipsis of the words, *namely, that is, to wit,* etc., takes place, the dash is used to supply them: "He excelled in three branches–arithmetic, algebra, and geometry."
7. A dash is used to denote the omission of part of a word when it is undesirable to write the full word: He is somewhat of a r—l (rascal). This is especially the case in profane words.
8. Between a citation and the authority for it there is generally a dash: "All the world's a stage."–Shakespeare.
9. When questions and answers are put in the same paragraph they should be separated by dashes:

"Are you a good boy? Yes, Sir.–Do you love study? I do."

Parenthesis

Marks of parenthesis (()) are used to separate expressions inserted in the body of a sentence, which are illustrative of the meaning, but have no essential connection with the sentence, and could be done without. They should be used as little as possible for they show that something is being brought into a sentence that does not belong to it.

1. *When the unity of a sentence is broken the words causing the break should be enclosed in parenthesis*: "We cannot believe a liar (and Jones is one), even when he speaks the truth."
2. *In reports of speeches marks of parenthesis are used to denote interpolations of approval or disapproval by the audience*: "The masses must not submit to the tyranny of the classes (hear, hear), we must show the trust magnates (groans), that they cannot ride rough-shod over our dearest rights (cheers);" "If the gentleman from Koc (Mr. Raman), will not be our spokesman, we must select another".

When a parenthesis is inserted in the sentence where no comma is required, no point should be used before either parenthesis. When inserted at a place requiring a comma, if the parenthetical matter relates to the whole sentence, a comma should be used before each parenthesis; if it relates to a single word, or short clause, no stop should come before it, but a comma should be put after the closing parenthesis.

Quotation Marks

The quotation marks are used to show that the words enclosed by them are borrowed.

1. A direct quotation should be enclosed within the quotation marks: Abraham Lincoln said,–"I shall make this land too hot for the feet of slaves."
2. When a quotation is embraced within another, the contained quotation has only single marks: Franklin said, "Most men come to believe 'honesty is the best policy.'"
3. When a quotation consists of several paragraphs the quotation marks should precede each paragraph.
4. Titles of books, pictures and newspapers when formally given are quoted.
5. Often the names of ships are quoted though there is no occasion for it.

Apostrophe

The Apostrophe (') should come under the comma rather than under the quotation marks or double comma. The word is Greek and signifies a turning away from. The letter elided or turned away is generally an *e*. In poetry and familiar dialogue the apostrophe marks the elision of a syllable, as "I've for I have"; "Thou'rt for thou art"; "you'll for you will," etc. Sometimes it is necessary to abbreviate a word by leaving out several letters. In such case the apostrophe takes the place of the omitted letters as "cont'd for continued."

The apostrophe is used to denote the elision of the century in dates, where the century is understood or to save the repetition of a series of figures, as "The Spirit of '76"; "I served in the army during the years 1895, '96, '97, '98 and '99." The principal use of the apostrophe is to denote the possessive case. All nouns in the singular number whether proper names or not, and all nouns in the plural ending with any other letter than *s*, form the possessive by the addition of the apostrophe and the letter *s*.

The only exceptions to this rule are, that, by poetical license the additional *s* may be elided in poetry for sake of the metre, and in the scriptural phrases "For goodness' sake." "For conscience' sake," "For Jesus' sake," etc. Custom has done away with the *s* and these phrases are now idioms of the language. All plural nouns ending in *s* form the possessive by the addition of the apostrophe only as boys', horses'. The possessive case of the personal pronouns never take the apostrophe, as ours, yours, hers, theirs.

CAPITALISATION

Capital letters are used to give emphasis to or call attention to certain words to distinguish them from the context. In manuscripts they may be written small or large and are indicated by lines drawn underneath, two lines for small capitals and three lines for capitals.

There are many rules to capitalisation. Most people know the basics of capitalisation such as capitalising first letter of the first word at the beginning of a new sentence, but when is capitalisation appropriate in other situations? Outlined below is a comprehensive guide providing rules and examples to proper capitalisation.

Use capital letters in the following ways:

– *The first words of a sentence*

When he tells a joke, he sometimes forgets the punch line.

– *The pronoun "I"*

The last time I visited Goa was several years ago.

– *Proper nouns (the names of specific people, places, organisations, and sometimes things)*

Coca Coal Company.

India Gate.

Supreme Court.

Janpath 10, New Delhi.

Indian Ocean.

– *Family relationships (when used as proper names)*

I sent a thank-you note to Aunt Amrutha, but not to my other aunts.

Here is a present I bought for Mother.

Did you buy a present for your mother?

– *The names of God, specific deities, religious figures, and holy books*

God the Father

the Virgin Mary

the *Quran*

the Greek gods

Moses

Shiva

Buddha

Krishna

– *Exception: Do not capitalise the non-specific use of the word "god."*

The word "polytheistic" means the worship of more than one god.

– *Titles preceding names, but not titles that follow names*

She worked as the assistant to Mayor Sonia.

I was able to interview Sheela Dutt, mayor of the city.

– *Directions that are names (North, South, East, and West when used as sections of the country, but not as compass directions)*

The Patels have moved to the Southwest.

Raju's house is two miles north of Haryana.

– *The days of the week, the months of the year, and holidays (but not the seasons used generally)*

October

Friday

Winter

Spring

Fall

– *Exception: Seasons are capitalised when used in a title.*

The Fall 2008 semester

– *The names of countries, nationalities, and specific languages*

Costa Rica

Hindi

French

English

– *The first word in a sentence that is a direct quote*

Emerson once said, "A foolish consistency is the hobgoblin of little minds."

– *The major words in the titles of books, articles, and songs (but not short prepositions or the articles "the," "a," or "an," if they are not the first word of the title)*

One of my's favourite books is *My Experiment with Truth.*

– *Members of national, political, racial, social, civic, and athletic groups*

Green Bay Packers

Indo-Americans

Japanese

Democrats

Friends of the Wilderness

Chinese

— *Periods and events (but not century numbers)*

Victorian Era

Great Depression

Constitutional Convention

Sixteenth century

— *Trademarks*

Pepsi

Honda

IBM

Microsoft Word

— *Words and abbreviations of specific names (but not names of things that came from specific things but are now general types)*

Freudian

NBC

Pasteurise

UN

french fries

Italics

7

Art of Letter Writing

Letter writing is an art. A well-written letter is always a pleasure to read. Writing a letter is about conveying a message. Letter writing is much different from other kind of writing. The context can be casual or formal. There are other essentials to be noted as to whom the letter is addressed and if there is any tone required in the language. The flow of thoughts has to be continual.

Receiving a letter from a loved one or a surprise connection is a pleasant feeling. Some letters also happen in a very easy language. Though formatting or indexing has to be followed, hand written letters are also well appreciated. Most letters today are in the electronic medium and hence a hand written letter has a personal touch.

Letters going to long distances need to be have the complete address and codes. One can receive the news of the birth of a new born, death of someone loved or also about a promotion. There are so many events in life that has to conveyed. A letter of condolence is a straight-from-heart emotion penned with lot of feelings.

The best way to say someone sorry is through a note. Keep the details brief. ' Am sorry to have hurt you.' This conveys the respect and love you have for the person.

'Thank you' letters can be expressed as, ' Thank you for attending my wedding.' 'Many thanks for your blessings.' There is not much formality required when writing to your sibling or parents.

Always make it a point to write the date in an indexed form. Formal letters require a subject line that has to be brief for e.g. Sub: EMI of my loan account or Sub: Disconnection of my internet. Keep the salutation very formal like Dear Sir, or Dear Ms. First names generally do not feature here. Sincerely is more preferred to 'yours faithfully' in formal letters.

Letters also serve as memories. Envelopes are important. A love note is cherished by the receiver and you could also use some fragrant paper or include some dried flowers in a string letter. Papers come in ecological and recycled quality. Printed or plain coloured ones is again a variety.

Make the letter clear and simple. Use short words, clear words as much as possible. Avoid jargon or vague words which may confuse the letter reader. Use only one side of the paper. Make your letter short. Be as brief as possible. Do not waste the reader precious time. Long letters are a turn-off.

Make your letter come alive. Try to address the letter directly to the reader. Visualise the reader ahead of you & and imagine yourself talking with him through your letter. Anyone would like to read a pleasant letter when it appears specially written for him.

Avoid spelling, poor grammar, and mistakes in your letter. If you can prepare your letter on a computer, it will be neater.

The principles of letter-writing should be understood by everybody who has any knowledge of written language, for almost everybody at some time or other has necessity to address some friend or acquaintance at a distance, whereas comparatively few are called upon to direct their efforts towards any other kind of composition.

Formerly the illiterate countryman, when he had occasion to communicate with friends or relations, called in the peripatetic schoolmaster as his amanuensis, but this had one draw-back,–secrets had to be poured into an ear other than that for which they were intended, and often the confidence was betrayed.

Now, that education is abroad in the land, there is seldom any occasion for any person to call upon the service of another to compose and write a personal letter. Very few nowadays are so grossly illiterate as not to be able to read and write. No matter how crude his effort may be it is better for any one to write his own letters than trust to another. Even if he should commence–"deer fren, i lift up my pen to let ye no that i hove been sik for the past 3 weeks, hopping this will findye the same," his spelling and construction can be excused in view of the fact that his intention is good, and that he is doing his best to serve his own turn without depending upon others.

The nature, substance and tone of any letter depend upon the occasion that calls it forth, upon the person writing it and upon the person for whom it is intended. Whether it should be easy or formal in style, plain or ornate, light or serious, gay or grave, sentimental or matter-of-fact depend upon these three circumstances.

In letter writing the first and most important requisites are to be natural and simple; there should be no straining after effect, but simply a spontaneous outpouring of thoughts and ideas as they naturally occur to the writer. We are repelled by a person who is stiff and laboured in his conversation and in the same way the stiff and laboured letter bores the reader. Whereas if it is light and in a conversational vein it immediately engages his attention.

The letter which is written with the greatest facility is the best kind of letter because it naturally expresses what is in the writer, he has not to search for his words, they flow in a perfect unison with the ideas he desires to communicate. When you write to your friend Rohit to tell him how you spent Sunday you have not to look around for the words, or study set phrases with a view to please or impress Rohit, you just tell him the same as if he were present before you, how you spent the day, where you were, with whom you associated and the chief incidents that occurred during the time. Thus, you write natural and it is such writing that is adapted to epistolary correspondence.

There are different kinds of letters, each calling for a different style of address and composition, nevertheless the natural key should be maintained in all, that is to say, the writer should never attempt to convey an impression that he is other than what he is. It would be silly as well as vain for the common street labourer of a limited education to try to put on literary airs and emulate a college professor; he may have as good a brain, but it is not as well developed by education, and he lacks the polish which society confers. Letters may be divided into those of friendship, acquaintanceship, those of business relations, those written in an official capacity by public servants, those designed to teach, and those which give accounts of the daily happenings on the stage of life, in other words, news letters.

Parts of the Letter

The art of writing a letter takes practice, knowledge about proper form and the ability to put into words the thoughts and feelings which are associated with the letter. Learning to write a letter can be difficult, as there are multiple types of letters which can written. To avoid the time that it may take to learn to write each one of these letters, if you are able to learn to write a basic letter, that will help you to create letters for a variety of occasions.

Your Address

At the top of your letter, you will put your address, so the reader will know where to send their reply to.

Date

Put the date on which the letter was written in the format Month, Day, Year i.e. June, 15, 2009.

Inside Address

The inside address is only required for a business letter and will include the address of the person you are writing to along with the name of the recipient, their title and company name. If you are not sure who the letter should be addressed to either leave it blank or try to put in a title, i.e. "Director of Human Resources".

The Greeting

The greeting will address the individual that the letter is being sent to. This is usually completed in the form of "Dear Anne" or "Hey Anne", for less formal letters.

The Introductory Paragraph

The first paragraph and will generally outline the purpose for the letter and the reason that the letter is being sent. This can address any issues that are outstanding and is used to set the tone for the entire rest of the letter. In this first paragraph, the summary of the letter can be found and the intentions which will be displayed through the rest of the letter should be outlined. From the first paragraph of the letter, the introductory paragraph, the individual should be able to note the tone of the letter.

The Body

The body of the letter will expand upon the introductory paragraph and the individual can extend their thoughts and feelings further when it comes to the letter. The body of the letter can be anywhere from multiple pages for personal letters, to one page or two pages for most business letters and other types of proposals.

The Closing

In the closing of the letter, the individual will close the letter and finish any thoughts that have been mentioned. The closing of the letter comes in various forms from yours truly, for those individuals that are familiar with one another, to a traditional sincerely which is a versatile closing that can be used in a variety of letters detailing many situations.

Letters of Friendship

Letters of friendship are the most common and their style and form depend upon the degree of relationship and intimacy existing between the writers and those addressed.

Between relatives and intimate friends the beginning and end may be in the most familiar form of conversation, either affectionate or playful. They should, however, never overstep the boundaries of decency and propriety, for it is well to remember that, unlike conversation, which only is heard by the ears for which it is intended, written words may come under eyes other than those for whom they were designed. Therefore, it is well never to write anything which the world may not read without detriment to your character or your instincts. You can be joyful, playful, jocose, give vent to your feelings, but never stoop to low language and, above all, to language savouring in the slightest degree of moral impropriety.

A friendly letter is a way of communicating between two people (sometimes more) who are usually well acquainted. There are many uses and reasons for writing a friendly letter, but usually friendly letters will consist of topics on a personal level. Friendly letters can either be printed or hand-written.

The friendly letter is typically less formal than that of a business letter. Usually the first paragraph of the body will consist of an introduction which will give the recipient an idea about you're writing to them with a short summary of the main topic of your letter. If you don't know the person you are writing to, you may want to introduce yourself in this introductory paragraph as well.

The next few paragraphs will usually consist of the message you want to get across along with any details you may want to convey.

The last paragraph will usually be the conclusion where you wrap everything up. You can sum up your main idea in this paragraph, thank the recipient for their time, wish the recipient well, and/or ask any questions.

Since friendly letters are less formal, you can feel free to write it however you like, but the above format is fairly common.

Friendly Letter Format

In the friendly letter format, your address, date, the closing, signature, and printed name are all indented to the right half of the page (how far you indent in is up to you as long as the heading and closing is lined up, use your own discretion and make sure it looks presentable). Also the first line of each paragraph is indented.

Friendly Letter Format

Return Address Line 1
Return Address Line 2

Date (Month, Day, Year)

Dear Name of Recipient,

Body Paragraph 1 ....
....

Body Paragraph 2...... ....
....

Body Paragraph 3........ ....
....

Closing (Sincerely...),
Signature

P.S.

Your Address

All that is needed is your street address on the first line and the city, state and zip on the second line. (Not needed if the letter is printed on paper with a letterhead already on it.)

Date

Put the date on which the letter was written in the format Month, Day, Year i.e. August 30, 2003. Skip a line between the date and the salutation.

Salutation

Usually starts out with Dear so and so, or Hi so and so. There is a comma after the end of the salutation (you can use an exclamation point also if there is a need for some emphasis).

Body

The body is where you write the content of the letter; the paragraphs should be single spaced with a skipped line between each paragraph. Skip 2 lines between the end of the body and the closing.

Closing

Let's the reader know that you are finished with your letter; usually ends with Sincerely, Sincerely yours, Thank you, and so on. Note that there is a comma after the end of the closing and only the first word in the closing is capitalised.

Signature

Your signature will go in this section, usually signed in black or blue ink with a pen. Skip a line after your signature and the P.S.

P.S.

If you want to add anything additional to the letter you write a P.S. (post script) and the message after that. You can also add a P.P.S after that and a P.P.P.S. after that and so on.

Sample Friendly Letter

F-63 IInd Floor
Yamuna Vihar, New Delhi-20
July 16, 2007

Dear Aarati,

It feels like such a long time since the last time I saw you. I know it's only been several weeks since I saw you. So far my summer has been great!

I spend all my weekends at the beach. I am getting a nice time and you can no longer say I am paler than you. I have been playing lots of volleyball, surfing and building a nice collection of sea shells. Just this past weekend I took second place in a sandcastle building contest!

On the weekdays I work. I drive an ice cream truck around and sell ice cream to the kids. It is so cool. It is a combination of the two things I love most, ice cream and kids. The pay isn't too great but I love the job so much.

I hope the summer's been going well for you too. There's only a month and a half left in summer vacation and after that it's back to school. Would you like to meet up some time to before school starts?

Your friend,

Signature

P.S. Shyam Karan says hi.

Business Letters

Business letters are of the utmost importance on account of the interests involved. The business character of a man or of a firm is often judged by the correspondence. On many occasions letters instead of developing trade and business interests and gaining clientele, predispose people unfavourably towards those whom they are designed to benefit. Ambiguous, slip-shod language is a detriment to success. Business letters should be clear, concise, to the point and, above all, honest, giving no wrong impressions or holding out any inducements that cannot be fulfilled. In business letters, just as in business conduct, honesty is always the best policy.

A business letter is a formal way of communicating between two or more parties. There are many different uses and business letters. Business letters can be informational, persuasive, motivational, or promotional. Business letters should be typed and printed out on standard 8.5″ x 11″ white paper.

Elements of a Good Business Letter

The most important element of writing a good letter is your ability to identify and write to your audience. If you are addressing your letter to the department of human resources, avoid using highly technical terms that only engineers would understand, even if your letter is addressed to an engineering company, chances are that the personnel in human resources does not have an engineering background.

The next element is that you make sure your present your objective in a clear and concise manner. Don't be vague about your objective, most people will not have the patience to sit there and guess at the meaning of your letter or the time to read a long-winded letter, just get to the point without going into unnecessary details.

Another important element to remember is to remain professional. Even if you are writing a complaint letter, remain polite and courteous, simply state the problem(s) along with any other relevant information and be sure to avoid threats and slander.

Business Letter Format

Block Format: Business Letter

Return Address Line 1
Return Address Line 2
Date (Month, Day, Year)

Mr./Mrs./Ms./Dr. Full name of recipient.
Title/Position of Recipient.
Company Name
Address Line 1
Address Line 2

Dear Ms./Mrs./Mr. Last Name:

Subject: Title of Subject

Body Paragraph 1 ....

Body Paragraph 2 ....

Body Paragraph 3 ....

Closing (Sincerely...),
Signature

Your Name (Printed)
Your Title

Enclosures (2)
Typist Initials.

The block format is the simplest format; all of the writing is flush against the left margin.

Your Address

The return address of the sender of the letter so the recipient can easily find out where to send a reply to. Skip a line between your address and the date.

Date

Put the date on which the letter was written in the format Month, Day, Year i.e. August 30, 2009. Skip a line between the date and the inside address (some people skip 3 or 4 lines after the date).

Inside Address

The address of the person you are writing to along with the name of the recipient, their title and company name, if you are not sure who the letter should be addressed to either leave it blank, but try to put in a title, i.e. "Director of Human Resources". Skip a line between the date and the salutation.

Salutation

Dear Ms./Mrs./Mr. Last Name:, Dear Director of Department Name: or To Whom It May Concern: if recipient's name is unknown. Note that there is a colon after the salutation. Skip a line between the salutation and the subject line or body.

Subject Line (optional)

Makes it easier for the recipient to find out what the letter is about. Skip a line between the subject line and the body.

Body

The body is where you write the content of the letter; the paragraphs should be single spaced with a skipped line between each paragraph. Skip a line between the end of the body and the closing.

Closing

Let's the reader know that you are finished with your letter; usually ends with Sincerely, Sincerely yours,

Thank you, and so on. Note that there is a comma after the end of the closing and only the first word in the closing is capitalised. Skip 3-4 lines between the closing and the printed name, so that there is room for the signature.

Signature

Your signature will go in this section, usually signed in black or blue ink with a pen.

Printed Name

The printed version of your name, and if desired you can put your title or position on the line underneath it. Skip a line between the printed name and the enclosure.

Enclosure

If letter contains other document other than the letter itself your letter will include the word "Enclosure." If there is more than one you would type, "Enclosures (#)" with the # being the number of other documents enclosed that doesn't include the letter itself.

Reference Initials

If someone other than yourself typed the letter you will include your initials in capital letters followed by the typist's initials in lower case in the following format; AG/gs or AG:gs.

Official Letters

Official letters are mostly always formal. They should possess clearness, brevity and dignity of tone to impress the receivers with the proper respect for the national laws and institutions.

Didactic Letters

Letters designed to teach or *didactic letters* are in a class all by themselves. They are simply literature in the form of letters and are employed by some of the best writers to give their thoughts and ideas a greater emphasis. The most conspicuous example of this kind of composition is the book on Etiquette by Lord Chesterfield, which took the form of a series of letters to his son.

News Letters

News letters are accounts of world happenings and descriptions of ceremonies and events sent into the newspapers. Some of the best authors of our time are newspaper men who write in an easy flowing style which is most readable, full of humour and fancy and which carries one along with breathless interest from beginning to end.

The principal parts of a letter are:

1. the *heading* or introduction;
2. the *body* or substance of the letter;
3. the *subscription* or closing expression and signature;
4. the *address* or direction on the envelope.

For the *body* of a letter no forms or rules can be laid down as it altogether depends on the nature of the letter and the relationship between the writer and the person addressed. There are certain rules which govern the other three features and which custom has sanctioned. Every one should be acquainted with these rules.

Letter Writing Tips

- Always proofread your letter after writing it, check for sentence structure, grammar, spelling mistakes

- Proofread your letter again (and again) after you have revised it.
- Keep the recipient in mind, and write in a way that he/she can easily understand the letter.
- Don't use abbreviated dates, i.e. use November 19, 2004, and not 11/19/04
- Be respectful when you write, even if you are writing a letter of complaint.

Presentation of the Letter

The presentation of the letter can be hand-written for less formal letters that are addressed to friends and family members, especially thank-you letters. In the case that you have illegible handwriting, you may want to consider typing the letter in these cases, although proper etiquette dictates against this type of behaviour.

Formal letters which are written on behalf of businesses to or professional contacts should remain typewritten and grammatical and spelling error free. These types of letters should be legible and professional and therefore typing the letter is one of the most effective ways to ensure that the letter demonstrates a professional appearance through the entire course of the letter, thereby creating a positive impression on the recipient of the letter.

As well as outward presentation, it is important to determine the tone which will be written in the letter, including a professional tone or a tone that will be taken with friends or family members in a more informal setting. The tone should be established from the greeting of the letter, into the introductory paragraph, throughout the entire body of the letter and even into the closing statement and closing greeting of the letter.

Read through the letter once it has been completed to ensure that the tone remains the same. The tone can be adjusted based on the language which is used through the letter, as well as the greetings (familiar as opposed to formal).

Addressing an Envelope

Addressing an envelope should be fairly simple. In the upper-left hand corner should be your name, and underneath that should be your return address. In the upper-right hand corner should be the postage stamp (with the correct postage amount). In the middle-centre should be the recipient's name and recipient's address.

Envelope Format

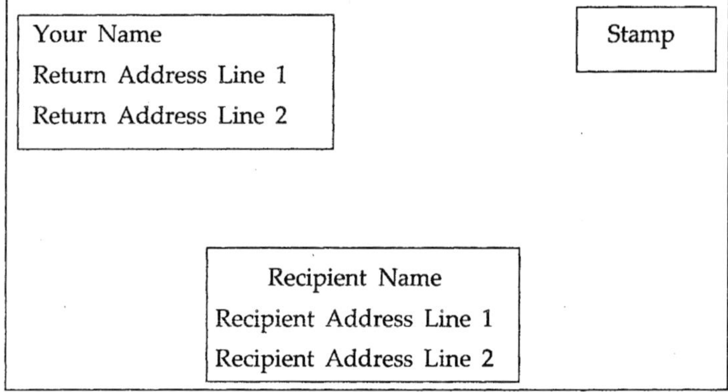

Tips

- Print/write all the information on the envelope before stuffing and sealing it so it will be written/printed on a flat surface.
- If you are writing to a different country, make sure you put it at on the last line of your return address

and the recipient's address. If you are writing a friendly letter with a small envelope, you can write the return address on the flap of the envelope if their is no room on the top-left hand corner.

E-MAILS

The following are some tips to help you when you are writing business letters through e-mail.

- A heading is not necessary in an e-mail (your return address, their address, and the date).
- Use a descriptive subject line.
- Avoid using an inappropriate or silly e-mail, register a professional sounding address if you don't have one.
- Use simple formatting, keep everything flush with the left margin; avoid special formatting and tabs.
- Keep your letter formal, just because it's an email instead of a hard copy is no excuse for informality (don't forget to use spell check and proper grammar).
- Try to keep your letter less than 80 characters wide, some e-mail readers will create line breaks on anything longer and ruin the formatting.
- If possible avoid attachments unless the recipient has requested or is expecting an attachment. If it is a text document, simply cut and paste the text below your letter and strip off any special formatting.
- If the persons name is unknown, address the person's title i.e. Dear Director of Human Resources.

E-mail Etiquette

E-mail etiquette is often a commonly overlooked part of the business and professional world despite being an important part of conveying a professional image. Emails written to friends and family will be less formal and will not need to follow any particular guidelines or rules, but when writing to someone at a professional level the following guidelines and rules should be taken into account.

- Use a descriptive subject line, avoid leaving it blank or putting an irrelevant or general subject.
- Address the recipient by name to add a personal touch to your letter.
- DO NOT USE ALL CAPS!
- Avoid over using punctuation marks!!!!!!!!!!!!
- Avoid using abbreviations, such as IMHO (in my humble opinion) or TTYL (talk to you later), not everyone is familiar with them.
- Skip a line when starting a new paragraph, avoid using tabs to signify a new paragraph, different email programmes read tabs in different ways.
- Avoid using HTML in your e-mails, not everyone can view it and it takes away from the professional image of the letter.
- If you are sending an attachment, make note of it and describe what the attachment is for in the body, some people are very wary of attachments due to the threat of computer viruses.
- Keep your emails as concise as possible without leaving out any important information.
- Keep usage of quoted text to a minimum.
- Always leave a signature line, don't assume the person already knows who you are.

- Do not keep on sending the same message to the same person over and over again, if they don't respond after a few days, send them an e-mail enquiring if they received your first e-mail.
- Use spell check and proof read and revise your letter after it's done.
- Use threads, if you get a message from someone and you are going to respond, don't send a new message, simply hit the reply option on your e-mail, this keeps the original subject line with "Re:" in front of it.
- If you are sending out an e-mail to a large private list don't use CC: (carbon copy) use BCC: (blind carbon copy) to protect the addresses of the recipients.
- Remember most e-mails are never completely private, there is always a chance of someone else besides the intended recipient reading it, so avoid writing any personal attacks which are unprofessional to begin with.
- When reading e-mails treat them as if they are private messages (unless you know you are allowed to share it with others).
- When you receive a message reply to it as soon as you have time to.

8

How to Speak English Fluently?

English is a widespread and important language in the world today. It is used for everything from international academic conferences to news reports to popular music lyrics. It is used not only for communication between native speakers and non-native speakers of English but between non-native speakers. Even though it does not have the greatest number of speakers in the world, it is the most widely used language in the world, and it will be used by more people in the future.

It is difficult to estimate exactly how many English speakers there are, but according to one estimate there are more than 350,000,000 native English speakers and more than 400,000,000 speakers of English as a second language. The importance of English is not just in how many people speak it but in what it is used for. English is the major language of news and information in the world. It is the language of business and government even in some countries where it is a minority language. Throughout the world, many professional papers are published in English. In India alone, there are three thousand magazines published in English. In many countries, television news is broadcast in English. Because of the power of television, demonstrators in every country use signs printed in English for the benefit of the international press.

English is a major language of international business, diplomacy, and science and the professions. It is the language that an Iranian businessman and a Japanese businessman are likely to use to communicate. Important commodities such as silver, tin, and hard currency are traded in English. English is also an official language, or the official language, of many international organisations, including the United Nations and many professional organisations. It is frequently the language of international conferences, and it is the language of international athletics.

Popular culture has also played an important part in spreading English. American and British popular music are heard all over the world. American movies are seen in almost every country. Books in English are available even in countries where few people actually use English. One reason that students give for learning English is to understand these songs, movies and books.

English is also very important for international travel. Much of the information countries disseminate about themselves outside of their borders is in English. English is spoken in large hotels and tourist attractions, at airports, and in shops that tourists frequent. Tours are almost always available in English. Even in countries where few people speak English on the street, people who work with tourists generally speak English.

To become a fluent English speaker, you must study and master reading, listening, and speaking. This chapter aims to help readers to learn how to speak English fluently. Using the tips provides in this chapter you will be able to learn English at a much faster speed.

Have a Good Dictionary

The first step to learning English is having a good dictionary. If you really want to improve your fluency with the language you should use an "English-English" dictionary. Many people find it comfortable using a "Hindi-English" or "Marathi-English" dictionary. Do "not" use this kind of dictionary. Use an "English-English" dictionary only!

There are many advantages of an English-English dictionary. In this kind of dictionary, the meanings are explained in English like:

> to criticise = to say negative things about; to talk about the mistakes of

So you have to understand the meaning of the meaning too. This helps you to familiarise your self with the language and also exposes you to new English words that you should find out the meanings of.

To really accelerate your English learning process, go in for an English-English dictionary. Not only should you have this kind of dictionary. You must also use it. Use it every time you come across a new word.

Keep in mind that when you buy your English-English dictionary, you buy a version that is for learners, not the version for native speakers. Usually, "students version" or "learners version" etc. will be written on the dictionary.

The most important thing that the dictionary you buy must contain:

— The dictionary that you buy "must" contain example sentences along with every word. For example: reaction: Response to an earlier activity.

  E.g. Sentence: What was your reaction when you heard the news?

Having an example sentence is very useful. Some times the meaning provided with the word may be a little confusing. So you may misunderstand what the word means. The sample sentence clears all such doubts.

Having a sample sentence is very important because it tells you how the word can be used in conjunction with other words. How the different words connect to form a sentence. Reading the sample sentence "programmes the brain" to use the word properly.

When you purchase a dictionary, make sure it has a lot of sample sentences. It would be even better if you purchase two different dictionaries with a lot of different sample sentences. This will give you a much better understanding of the word you look up.

The best way to use the sample sentences in the dictionary is to learn them. Whenever you are looking up some new word and you come across a sample sentence, you must read it again and again until you know the sentence by-heart.

If you do this, you will be in a position to use the word or the phrase in sentences of your own correctly. Forming correct sentences becomes easy if you learn the sample sentences after reading them again and again.

Nowadays, many dictionaries, come with a CD. These CD's contain the software version of the dictionary. This is especially convenient if you have easy access to a computer. You don't have to waste too much time looking for the word you want. It is quite easy to look it up using the software dictionary. Also, the software dictionary may have audio files for the words. These audio files can be played and the correct pronunciation for a word can be known. Try to look out for a dictionary that comes along with this kind of CD.

There are many online dictionaries available. They too allow you to search for any word conveniently. Some of them even provide audio files containing pronunciations of all the different words.

When you go to buy your dictionary, look out for these things:

- It's an English-English dictionary.
- It's a students or learners version.
- It has a lot of sample sentences.
- It comes with a CD that is a software dictionary and preferably has pronunciations for the words.

Getting Inputs

It is said quite often that you should practice talking in English or you will not learn. However, this has a "very bad" effect if you do not have sufficient input of English.

If you do not have sufficient input, the sentences you form will be wrong. If these sentences formed are wrong, and no one corrects you, you will start to think that what you have said is correct. Because of this, your mind will be filled with wrong English sentences. Everything you say, all the sentences you form will be incorrect.

So, if you want to practice talking in English, you "must" make sure that the people around you will be in a position to correct you as soon as you make the mistake. If you want to practice speaking in English, you have to speak English correctly. If you speak incorrectly you "must know" that you have spoken incorrectly.

Unfortunately, most English learners do not have native English speakers around them who will always correct them when they go wrong. In this case, it is wise to first get enough input of the language before you "utter even the first word."

Input is basically any correct English that you may hear or read. If you listen to an English radio station, that is input. If you read a book, then that is input. If you hear to fluent English speakers talking then that is input. If a fluent English speaker is talking to you in English then that is input. All languages are learnt mainly by input. It is the fastest and the best way of learning a language!

When you were a baby you naturally learnt your mother tongue because of all the input of the language from you parents and surroundings. The human brain learns by imitation. When you hear a sentence it gets stored in your brain. When you want to say the same thing or some thing that is similar, you imitate the sentence that is stored in your brain.

Consider the sentence:

Ram runs much faster than Rahim.

Assume that this sentence is given as input. Later when you want to say a similar thing, your brain pulls this sentence out of your memory and comes up with:

Hesham runs much faster than Ram.

or

Sharmila runs much slower than Leela. etc.

Basically, learning is done by imitation! Input is what is fed into the brain so that there is something available for imitation. The more the input, more sentences are available for the brain to imitate.

So the fastest way of learning how to speak the language fluently would be to get as much as possible input of the language. The more input of the language you get the more correct sentences you will be able to form when you try to speak the language.

You must try to get "as much as possible" input of correct English. The more input you get the more sentences you will be able to form correctly. The more sentences you can form correctly the more your confidence of speaking English will increase and the more you will learn!

There is English input available everywhere. Here are a few tips and suggestions for you to find input of English around you and improve your English speech:

Rent/Buy an English DVD

Rent or buy an English movie DVD. Put the English subtitles on. Follow the movie.

This has many advantages:

1. You will be able to compare the written words to the correct pronunciations.
2. You will get a feel of how real English sentences are formed when speaking.
3. You will be learning English but it will not be frustrating and boring because you will be watching a movie.

When you watch the movie be sure to keep your dictionary handy. Whenever you come across a new word, pause the movie and look it up in the dictionary. If you don't do this, the whole experience will be quite pointless.

Read

There are a lot of English magazines available on a lot of different topics. No matter what subject interests you, there must be some magazine that talks about it. There are English magazines about Business, Brides, House Keeping, Stock Market, Sports, Computers, Electronics, Linux, Graphic Designing, Cooking etc.Find the magazine that interests you and read it cover to cover. Be sure to look out for new words and new phrases and look them up in the dictionary as you go.

Read English fiction of your choice. This is our India. Books are not costly here. You get cheap book in every nook and corner. Pick up some thing that interests you.

Take it home and read it. Be sure to look up all the new words you come across in the book.

If you cannot find a book or magazine of your choice, look for information you are interested in on the Internet. There is information available on every topic under the sun on the Internet.

Read Internet Forums

Got to Internet forums of the subject matter that interests you. Generally most of the forums are in English language and are a great source of English input.

For those of you who are not familiar with Internet forums, these are places where people interested in a particular subject can get together and share their views and opinions about a particular subject. You can also ask specific questions to other people and they will help you out if they can. On the Internet, there are forums available about each and every subject.

Forums are a great source of information. Also in forums real people talk about real problems. Most of the information typed in forums is written in an informal way. Because of this the forums make a good source for English input. Reading forums exposes you to a lot of phrases of daily use. When reading forums also make sure you find out the meaning of every new word or phrase you come across or the whole exercise will be useless.

Listen to the Radio and TV

The "All India Radio" has some good programmes that are designed to teach English to the listener. Besides this, there are also many different radio stations available nowadays in the big cities. Some of these radio stations are in English. Listen to them to get a feel of the language.

Besides the radio, you could also listen to the "News In English". It's available on a wide variety of channels. The news is a good place to get input of the English language because it is spoken in a very clear, easy to understand way.

Chat with Fluent English speakers

Chat with fluent English speakers real or online. Make friends with interesting English speakers. Become pen-pals with a fluent English speaker. While talking to them look at their lip movement for tips on how to pronounce words correctly.

Think in English

One of the most common mistakes that English learners make is, they think in their mother tongue. When they want to say something in English, they think in their mother tongue, translate it to English and then say it in English. The result is a very flawed English sentence. Never do this. If you want to speak in English fluently you will have to learn to "think" in English. When you are constructing sentences in your mind before saying them, think in English and form them in English in your mind.

TELEPHONING

Learning how to communicate well on the telephone is one of the top priorities for many students who need to use English at work. Learning the common phrases that are used on the telephone helps students know what to expect. However, what students often need most is practice, practice, and more practice. While helpful, practising a role-play in the classroom is not always the best way to improve telephoning skills.

Telephoning requires special skills as there are a number of difficulties that arise when telephoning that are specific to telephoning. The first and foremost difficulty is not being able to see the person you are communicating with. This lack of visual communication often makes students, who can communicate quite successfully in other situations, nervous and thereby hinders their communicative abilities. Add to this the typical hectic pace of business communication, and you have a particularly difficult situation.

This feature includes a number of ingredients to improve telephoning skills. Included you will find specific telephoning phrases, telephoning techniques to improve confidence when telephoning and telephoning practice exercises for use with your colleagues or in the classroom.

The fear of talking on the phone in a second language will disappear if you practise often. The hardest part about using the phone in a language that is not your own is the fact that you cannot see the other person's eyes, mouth and body movements. Although you might not be aware of it, in face-to-face conversation you lip-read and watch for smiles, frowns and moving hands. Listening to someone on the telephone is like doing a section from a taped recording in class.

Telephonic Phrases

There are a number of phrases and idioms that are only used when telephoning. Let's first take a look at an example dialogue. Here are the most common:

Operator: Hello, Jai and Brothers, How can I help you?

Nitin: This is Nitin Aggarwal. Can I have extension 3421?

Operator: Certainly, hold on a minute, I'll put you through...

Rahul: Jai and Brothers's office, Rahul speaking.

Nitin: This is Nitin Aggarwal calling, is Jai in?

Rahul: I'm afraid he's out at the moment. Can I take a message?

Nitin: Yes, Could you ask him to call me at. I need to talk to him about the Nuovo line, it's urgent.

Rahul: Could you repeat the number please?

Nitin: Yes, that's, and this is Nitin Aggarwal

Rahul: Thank you Mr Nitin, I'll make sure Jai gets this asap.

Nitin: Thanks, bye.

Rahuli: Bye.

As you can see, the language is rather informal and there are some important differences to everyday English. Look at the chart below for key language and phrases used in telephone English:

Introducing yourself

This is Sheela.

Sheela speaking

Asking who is on the telephone

Excuse me, who is this?

Can I ask who is calling, please?

Asking for Someone

- Can I have extension 321? (extensions are internal numbers at a company)
- Could I speak to...? (Can I - more informal / May I - more formal)
- Is Jai in? (informal idiom meaning: Is Jai in the office?

Connecting Someone

- I'll put you through (put through - phrasal verb meaning 'connect')

– Can you hold the line? Can you hold on a moment?

How to reply when someone is not available

– I'm afraid... is not available at the moment
– The line is busy... (when the extension requested is being used)
– Mr Jai isn't in... Mr Jai is out at the moment...

Taking a Message

– Could (Can, May) I take a message?
– Could (Can, May) I tell him who is calling?
– Would you like to leave a message?

Telephone Tips

1. *Speak slowly and clearly:* Listening to someone speaking in a second language over the telephone can be very challenging because you cannot see the person you are trying to hear. However, it may be even more difficult for the person you are talking with to understand you. You may not realise that your pronunciation isn't clear because your teacher and fellow students know and understand you. Pay special attention to your weak areas (such as "r's" and "l's" or "b's" and "v's") when you are on the phone. If you are nervous about using the phone in English, you may notice yourself speaking very quickly. Practise or write down what you are going to say and take a few deep breaths before you make a phone call.
2. *Make sure you understand the other speaker:* Don't pretend to understand everything you hear over the telephone. Even native speakers ask each other to repeat and confirm information from time to time. This is especially important if you are

taking a message for someone else. Learn the appropriate expressions that English speakers use when they don't hear something properly. Don't be afraid to remind the person to slow down more than once. Keep your telephone in an area that is away from other noise distractions such as a radio or television.

3. *Practise with a friend* : Ask another student to practise talking on the phone with you. You might choose one night a week and take turns phoning each other at a certain time. Try to talk for at least fifteen minutes. You can talk socially, or role play different scenarios in a business environment. If you don't have access to a telephone, you can practise by setting two chairs up back to back. The most important thing about practising telephone English is that you aren't able to see each other's mouths. It is amazing how much people lip-read without realising.

4. *Use businesses and recordings:* There are many ways to get free telephone English practice. After business hours, you can call and listen to recorded messages. Write down what you hear the first time, and then call back and check if your notes are accurate. Use the phone in your everyday life. Call for a pizza delivery instead of going out to eat. Call a salon to book a hair appointment. You can even phone the movie theatre to ask for the listings instead of using the newspaper. Some large cities have free recordings you can call for information such as your daily horoscope or the weather. Some products have free phone numbers on the packaging that you can call for information. Think of a question you might want to ask and call the free number! For example, call the number on the back of the cereal box and ask for coupons. You

will have to give your name and address. Make sure you have a pen handy so that you can repeat the information and check your comprehension.

Telephone Etiquette

The telephone; it is part of us. What would we do without it? It is as common as apple pie and summer sunshine. As much a part of our lives as learning to walk and talk and perhaps that is why we, at most times, give it little thought. Nonetheless, we do think about it, when we have had the experience of being treated rudely or abruptly while using this mode of communication. We bristle at the idea of someone's brusqueness to us, and most probably never take thought of the times we have shown our bad manners while speaking on the telephone.

The tendency to be short and curt to salespersons is common. The feeling that they are, in fact, invading our privacy is a widespread notion and the fist inclination is to cut them off with a positive projection of irritation. Perhaps supposing this will discourage any return calls, "wish on!" Treating those person who call pitching a product without kindness, solves nothing and makes no validity, so why not include them in you simple and polite response, "no thank you, have a good day," "good-bye." This response is much less apt to raise your blood pressure and reduce your feelings of guilt later, for incivility over the telephone.

Correct way to answer the telephone

The proper way to answer the telephone is "hello." On the other hand, simply answering "yes" is a curt and inappropriate response. The person making the call draws a very quick conclusion, and that is, to think of that person as cold and aloof, and hesitate to communicate readily.

At times, someone other than the head of the house will answer the telephone. If that person is asked, "may I speak to Mr. ________ please," the response should be, "one moment please, I will get him for you." If the head of household is not available the response should be, "I am sorry, Mr. _____ is not available at this time, may I take a message?" This is simply a form of good manners, whatever form it may be expressed, thoughtfulness for the feelings of others. This person may be calling to offer a new job with great pay and benefits, who's to know! What would he or she think if the answer to the question, "is Mr. _____ home please," would be an abrupt "no." This response would reflect negatively, on the actual person being called.

Making telephone calls:

Think about what time it is, when placing a call. You would not want to call when there is the possibility that person may be asleep. For example on a work morning before 7:00 a.m. would not be a good time. After 9:00 to 10:00 p.m. in the evening is not a good time, and remember to avoid calls around the usual period most people will be eating. Courtesy is expected when using the telephone just as if you are talking in person.

Give your name when the telephone is answered, before asking for the person you are requesting.

Dialing too quickly, or in inadequate lighting may be the cause of dialing a "wrong number," never just hang-up. Express your apology, letting them know you have dialed a wrong number. To avoid disturbing another person unnecessarily dial carefully and make sure you can see the dial pad.

When speaking, think of the way you sound. Make sure you enunciate you words clearly and precisely. It is embarrassing to be asked to repeat what you are saying.

Your voice reflects your courtesy, since that person on the other end of the line cannot see your facial expressions your "tone of voice" will need to express this.

Basic Good Manners, Telephone Tips:

– Let the telephone ring a reasonable length of time. It is frustrating to just get to the telephone and hear a dial tone.

– If you dial a number that is wrong, apologize, promptly and hang-up.

– Calling a business at or very near closing time is to say the least un-thoughtful. When it is time to go home, after a long day, do not delay them.

– State your name when placing a call. The game of "guess who this is" may not play very well to a busy friend.

– When speaking to anyone who is working and time is of the essence, make your call informative and short.

– Dial carefully and in proper lighting to avoid calling a wrong number and in-conveniencing others.

9

English Pronunciation

English evolved from the Germanic languages brought to Britain by the Angles, Saxons, Jutes and other Germanic tribes, which are known collectively as Anglo-Saxon or Old English. Old English began to appear in writing during the early 8th century AD. Approximately 341 million people speak English as a native language and a further 267 million speak it as a second language in over 104 countries including the UK, Ireland, USA, Canada, Australia, New Zealand, South Africa, American Samoa, Andorra, Anguilla, Antigua and Barbuda, Aruba, Bahamas, Barbados, Belize, Bermuda, Botswana, British Indian Ocean Territory, British Virgin Islands, Brunei, Cameroon, Canada, Cayman Islands, Cook Islands and Denmark.

Pronouncing every word correctly leads to poor pronunciation. Good pronunciation comes from stressing the right words—this is because English is a time-stressed language. Always remember that English is not "phonetic". That means that we do not always say a word the same way that we spell it.

Some words can have the same spelling but different pronunciation, for example:

I like to read [ri:d].

I have read [red] that book.

Some words have different spelling but the same pronunciation, for example:

I have read [red] that book.

My favourite colour is red [red].

Sounds

The English language may have 26 letters of the alphabet, but it has double that number of sounds: 44. Knowing and recognising the 44 sounds will help to give you good pronunciation. We call these sounds phonemes. Of course, everybody knows that good pronunciation helps our speaking.

If you're concentrating on the sounds of English, there are 44 characters to represent them all. One way of doing this is to use the 'phonemic alphabet', which has some extra characters to represent the sounds in English for which there is no clear equivalent letter or letters.

The following lists provides you with sample words to teach the sounds in the English language.

The 5 Short Vowel Sounds

short -a- in and, as, after short -e- in pen, hen, lend

short -i- in it, in

short -o- in top, hop

short -u- in under, cup

The 6 Long Vowel Sounds

long -a- in make, take

long -e- in beet, feet

long -i- in tie, lie

long -o- in coat, toe

long -u- (yoo) in rule

long -oo- in few, blue

The R-Controlled Vowel Sounds

-ur- in her, bird, and hurt

-ar- in bark, dark

-or- in fork, pork, stork

The 18 Consonant Sounds

c, q and x are missing as they are found in other sounds. The C sound is found in the k sounds and in the s sound in words like cereal, city and cent. The Q sound is found in 'kw' words like backwards and Kwanza. The X sound is also found in ks words like kicks.

-b- in bed, bad

-k- in cat and kick

-d- in dog

-f- in fat

-g- in got

-h- in has

-j- in job

-l- in lid

-m- in mop

-n- in not

-p- in pan

-r- in ran

-s- in sit

-t- in to

-v- in van

-w- in went

-y- in yellow

-z- in zipper

The Blends

Blends are 2 or 3 letters combined to form a distinct spelling sound. The blends sounds:

-bl- in blue and black
-c- in clap and close
-fl- in fly and flip
-gl- in glue and glove
-pl- in play and please
-br- in brown and break
-cr- in cry and crust
-dr- in dry and drag
-fr- in fry and freeze
-gr- in great and grand
-pr- in prize and prank
-tr- in tree and try
-sk- in skate and sky
-sl- in slip and slap
-sp- in spot and speed
-st- in street and stop
-sw- in sweet and sweater
-spr- in spray and spring
-str- in stripe and strap

The 7 Digraph Sounds

-ch- in chin and ouch
-sh- in ship and push
-th- in thing
-th- in this
-wh- in when
-ng- in ring
-nk- in rink

Other Special Sounds Including Dipthongs

-oi- in foil and toy
-ow- in owl and ouch
short -oo- in took and pull
-aw- in raw and haul
-zh- in vision

PHONEMES

You can use phonemes to write out the pronunciation of words and in many dictionaries for English learners you will see the pronunciation written out. To show that what is written are phonemes (sounds) and not letters phonemic transcriptions are written between slashes, / /. For example, the pronunciation of the word 'pet' is written:/pet/ There are different kinds of sounds, consonants and vowels.

Phoneme is a group of slightly different sounds which are all perceived to have the same function by speakers of the language or dialect in question. An example of a phoneme is the /k/ sound in the words *kit* and *skill.* Even though most native speakers don't notice this, in most dialects, the *k* sounds in each of these words are actually pronounced differently: they are different *speech sounds,* or *phones* (which, in transcription, are placed in square brackets). In our example, the /k/ in *kit* is aspirated, [k^h], while the /k/ in *skill* is not, [k]. The reason why these different sounds are nonetheless considered to belong to the same phoneme in English is that if an English-speaker used one instead of the other, the meaning of the word would not change: saying [k^h] in *skill* might sound odd, but the word would still be recognised.

By contrast, some other sounds could be substituted which would cause a change in meaning, producing words like *still* (substituting /t/), *spill* (substituting /p/) and *swill* (substituting /w/). These other sounds (/t/, /p/ and /w/) are, in English, different phonemes. In some languages, however, [k^h] and [k] are different phonemes, and are perceived as such by the speakers of those languages. Thus, in Icelandic, /k^h/ is the first sound of *kátur* 'cheerful', while /k/ is the first sound of *gátur* 'riddles'.

In some languages, each letter in the spelling system represents one phoneme. However, in English spelling there is a poor match between spelling and phonemes.

Phones that belong to the same phoneme, such as [t] and [t^h] for English /t/, are called allophones. A common test to determine whether two phones are allophones or separate phonemes relies on finding minimal pairs: words that differ by only the phones in question.

Some linguists consider phonemes to be further decomposable into features, such features being the true minimal constituents of language. Features overlap each other in time, as do suprasegmental phonemes in oral language and many phonemes in sign languages. Features could be designated as acoustic or articulatory in nature.

Received Pronunciation

Received Pronunciation (RP) is a form of pronunciation of the English language which has traditionally been the prestige British accent. RP is a form of English English (English English is a term that has been applied to the English language as spoken in England), sometimes defined as the "educated spoken English of southeastern England." It is often taught to non-native speakers; used as the standard for English in most books on general phonology and phonetics; and represented in the pronunciation schemes of most British dictionaries.

RP is an accent and a register, rather than a dialect. It may show a great deal about the social and educational background of a person who uses English. Anyone using the RP will typically speak Standard English although the reverse is not necessarily true. RP is often believed to be based on the Southern accents of England, but in fact it has most in common with the Early Modern English dialects of the East Midlands. This was the most populated and most prosperous area of England during the 14th and 15th centuries. By the end of the 15th century, "Standard English" was established in the City of London. A mixture of London speech with elements from East Midlands, Middlesex and Essex, became known as RP.

. Researchers generally distinguish between three different forms of RP: Conservative, General, and Advanced. Conservative RP refers to a traditional accent associated with older speakers with certain social backgrounds; General RP is often considered neutral regarding age, occupation, or lifestyle of the speaker; and Advanced RP refers to speech of a younger generation of British speakers.

Traditionally, Received Pronunciation was the everyday speech in the families of Southern English persons whose men-folk have been educated at the great public boarding-schools and which conveys no information about that speaker's region of origin prior to attending the school. It is the business of educated people to speak so that no-one may be able to tell in what county their childhood was passed.

From the 1970s onwards, attitudes towards Received Pronunciation have been changing slowly. One of the catalysts for this was the influence in the 1960s of Harold Wilson, a Labour Prime Minister. Unusually for a Prime Minister, he spoke with elements of a Yorkshire accent. The BBC's use of announcers with strong regional accents during and after World War II is an earlier example of the use of non-RP accents.

The modern style of RP is an accent often taught to non-native speakers learning British English. Non-RP Britons abroad may modify their pronunciation to something closer to Received Pronunciation in order to be understood better by people unfamiliar with British regional accents. They may also modify their vocabulary and grammar to be closer to Standard English, for the same reason. RP is used as the standard for English in most books on general phonology and phonetics and is represented in the pronunciation schemes of most dictionaries.

Word Stress

Word stress is your magic key to understanding spoken English. Native speakers of English use word stress naturally. Word stress is so natural for them that they don't even know they use it. Non-native speakers who speak English to native speakers without using word stress, encounter two problems:

- They find it difficult to understand native speakers, especially those speaking fast.
- The native speakers may find it difficult to understand them.

To understand word stress, it helps to understand syllables. Every word is made from syllables. Each word has one, two, three or more syllables.

Word		Number of syllables
dog	dog	1
green	green	1
quite	quite	1
quiet	qui-et	2
orange	or-ange	2
table	ta-ble	2
expensive	ex-pen-sive	3
interesting	in-ter-est-ing	4
realistic	re-al-is-tic	4
unexceptional	un-ex-cep-tion-al	5

Notice that (with a few rare exceptions) every syllable contains at least one vowel (a, e, i, o or u) or vowel sound.

In English, we do not say each syllable with the same force or strength. In one word, we accentuate ONE syllable. We say one syllable very loudly (big, strong, important) and all the other syllables very quietly.

Let's take three words: photograph, photographer and photographic. Do they sound the same when spoken? No. Because we accentuate (stress) ONE syllable in each word. And it is not always the same syllable. So the shape of each word is different.

	total syllables	stressed syllable
PHO TO GRAPH	3	#1
PHO TO GRAPH ER	4	#2
PHO TO GRAPH IC	4	#3

This happens in ALL words with 2 or more syllables: TEACHer, JaPAN, INDIa, aBOVE, converSAtion, INteresting, imPORtant, deMAND, etCETera.

The syllables that are not stressed are weak or small or quiet. Native speakers of English listen for the STRESSED syllables, not the weak syllables. If you use word stress in your speech, you will instantly and automatically improve your pronunciation and your comprehension.

Try to hear the stress in individual words each time you listen to English—on the radio, or in films for example. Your first step is to HEAR and recognise it. After that, you can USE it.

There are two very important rules about word stress:

One word, one stress. (One word cannot have two stresses. So if you hear two stresses, you have heard two words, not one word.)

The stress is always on a vowel.

Word stress is not used in all languages. Some languages, Japanese or French for example, pronounce each syllable with eq-ual em-pha-sis.

Other languages, English for example, use word stress.

Word stress is not an optional extra that you can add to the English language if you want. It is part of the language! English speakers use word stress to communicate rapidly and accurately, even in difficult conditions. If, for example, you do not hear a word clearly, you can still understand the word because of the position of the stress.

Think again about the two words photograph and photographer. Now imagine that you are speaking to somebody by telephone over a very bad line. You cannot hear clearly. In fact, you hear only the first two syllables of one of these words, photo... Which word is it, photograph or photographer? Of course, with word stress you will know immediately which word it is because in reality you will hear either PHOto... or phoTO... So without hearing the whole word, you probably know what the word is (PHOto...graph or phoTO...grapher). It's magic!

This is a simple example of how word stress helps us understand English. There are many, many other examples, because we use word stress all the time, without thinking about it. There are some rules about which syllable to stress. But, the rules are rather complicated! Probably the best way to learn is from experience. Listen carefully to spoken English and try to develop a feeling for the "music" of the language.

When you learn a new word, you should also learn its stress pattern. If you keep a vocabulary book, make a note to show which syllable is stressed. If you do not know, you can look in a dictionary. All dictionaries give the phonetic spelling of a word. This is where they show which syllable is stressed, usually with an apostrophe (') just before or just after the stressed syllable.

Rules of Word Stress in English

There are two very simple rules about word stress:

1. One word has only one stress. (One word cannot have two stresses. If you hear two stresses, you hear two words. Two stresses cannot be one word. It is true that there can be a "secondary" stress in some words. But a secondary stress is much smaller than the main stress, and is only used in long words.)
2. We can only stress vowels, not consonants.

Here are some more, rather complicated, rules that can help you understand where to put the stress. But do not rely on them too much, because there are many exceptions. It is better to try to "feel" the music of the language and to add the stress naturally.

1 Stress on first syllable

Rule	*Example*
Most 2-syllable nouns	PRESent, EXport, CHIna, TAble
Most 2-syllable adjectives	PRESent, SLENder, CLEVer, HAPpy

2 Stress on last syllable

Rule	*Example*
Most 2-syllable verbs	to preSENT, to exPORT, to deCIDE, to beGIN

There are many two-syllable words in English whose meaning and class change with a change in stress. The word present, for example is a two-syllable word. If we stress the first syllable, it is a noun (gift) or an adjective (opposite of absent). But if we stress the second syllable, it becomes a verb (to offer). More examples: the words export, import, contract and object can all be nouns or verbs depending on whether the stress is on the first or second syllable.

3 Stress on penultimate syllable (penultimate = second from end)

Rule	*Example*
Words ending in -ic	GRAPHic, geoGRAPHic, geoLOGic
Words ending in -sion and -tion	teleVIsion, reveLAtion

For a few words, native English speakers don't always "agree" on where to put the stress. For example, some people say teleVIsion and others say TELevision. Another example is: CONtroversy and conTROversy.

4 Stress on ante-penultimate syllable (ante-penultimate = third from end)

Rule	*Example*
Words ending in -cy, -ty, -phy and -gy	deMOcracy, dependaBIlity, phoTOgraphy, geOLogy
Words ending in -al	CRItical, geoLOGical

5 Compound words (words with two parts)	
Rule	*Example*
For compound nouns, the stress is on the first part	BLACKbird, GREENhouse
For compound adjectives, the stress is on the second part	bad-TEMpered, old-FASHioned
For compound verbs, the stress is on the second part	to underSTAND, to overFLOW

Sentence Stress

Sentence stress is the music of spoken English. Like word stress, sentence stress can help you to understand spoken English, especially when spoken fast.

Sentence stress is what gives English its rhythm or "beat". You remember that word stress is accent on one syllable within a word. Sentence stress is accent on certain words within a sentence.

Most sentences have two types of word:

— content words

— structure words

Content words are the key words of a sentence. They are the important words that carry the meaning or sense.

Structure words are not very important words. They are small, simple words that make the sentence correct grammatically. They give the sentence its correct form or "structure".

If you remove the structure words from a sentence, you will probably still understand the sentence.

If you remove the content words from a sentence, you will not understand the sentence. The sentence has no sense or meaning.

Imagine that you receive this telegram message:

Will you SELL my CAR because I've GONE to FRANCE

This sentence is not complete. It is not a "grammatically correct" sentence. But you probably understand it. These 4 words communicate very well. *Somebody wants you to sell their car for them because they have gone to France.* We can add a few words:

Will you SELL my CAR because I've GONE to FRANCE

The new words do not really add any more information. But they make the message more correct grammatically. We can add even more words to make one complete, grammatically correct sentence. But the information is basically the same:

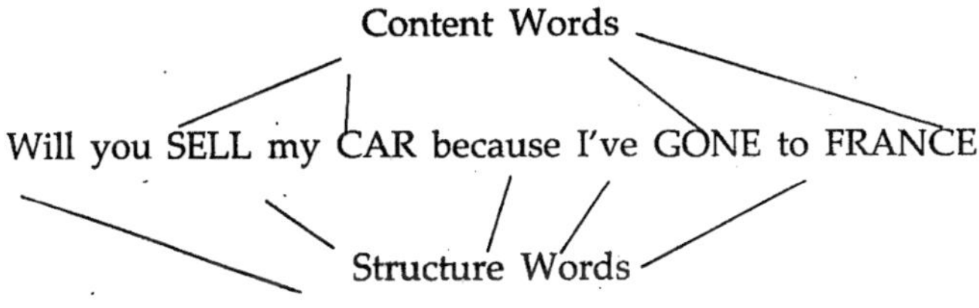

In our sentence, the 4 key words (sell, car, gone, France) are accentuated or stressed.

Why is this important for pronunciation? It is important because it adds "music" to the language. It is the rhythm of the English language. It changes the speed at which we speak (and listen to) the language. The time between each stressed word is the same.

In our sentence, there is 1 syllable between SELL and CAR and 3 syllables between CAR and GONE. But the time (*t*) between SELL and CAR and between CAR and GONE is the same. We maintain a constant beat on the stressed words. To do this, we say "my" more slowly, and "because I've" more quickly. We change the speed of the small structure words so that the rhythm of the key content words stays the same.

Rules for Sentence Stress in English

The basic rules of sentence stress are:

1. content words are stressed
2. structure words are unstressed
3. the time between stressed words is always the same

The following tables can help you decide which words are content words and which words are structure words:

Content words - stressed

Words carrying the meaning	Example
main verbs	sell, give, employ
nouns	car, music, mary
adjectives	red, big, interesting
adverbs	quickly, loudly, never
negative auxiliaries	don't, aren't, can't

Structure words - unstressed

Words for correct grammar	Example
pronouns	he, we, they
prepositions	on, at, into
articles	a, an, the
conjunctions	and, but, because
auxiliary verbs	do, be, have, can, must

The above rules are for for what is called "neutral" or normal stress. But sometimes we can stress a word that would normally be only a structure word, for example to correct information. Look at the following dialogue:

"They've been to Mongolia, haven't they?"

"No, THEY haven't, but WE have.

Note also that when "be" is used as a main verb, it is usually unstressed (even though in this case it is a content word).

PRONOUNCING HOMOPHONES

Homophones are words that have exactly the same sound (pronunciation) but different meanings and (usually) spelling.

For example, the following two words have the same sound, but different meanings and spelling:

The word homophone is made from two combining forms:

- homo- (from the Greek word "homos", meaning "same"
- -phone (from the Greek word "phone", meaning "voice" or "sound"

You will see many other English words using one or other of these combining forms.

The following list of 70 groups of homophones contains only the most common homophones, using relatively well-known words. These are headwords only. No inflections (such as third person singular "s" or noun plurals) are included.

air	heir
aisle	isle
ante-	anti-
eye	I
be	bee
brake	break
buy	by

cell	sell
cent	scent
cereal	serial
coarse	course
complement	compliment
dam	damn
dear	deer
die	dye
fair	fare
fir	fur
flour	flower
for	four
hair	hare
heal	heel
hear	here
him	hymn
hole	wholc
hour	our
idle	idol
in	inn
knight	night
knot	not
know	no
made	maid
mail	male
meat	meet
morning	mourning
none	nun
oar	or
one	won
pair	pear
peace	piece
plain	plane

poor	pour
pray	prey
principal	principle
profit	prophet
real	reel
right	write
root	route
sail	sale
sea	see
seam	seem
sight	site
shore	sure
sole	soul
some	sum
son	sun
stair	stare
stationary	stationery
steal	steel
suite	sweet
tail	tale
their	there
toe	tow
waist	waste
wait	weight
way	weigh
weak	week
wear	where

In a few cases, a third homophone, although possible, has not been included for simplicity. Different varieties and accents of English may produce variations in some of these pronunciations. The homophones listed here are based on British English.

Pronunciation of Vowels

Vowels are letters that are pronounced by forcing air over your vocal cords through your mouth. It is the shape of your mouth that decides which vowel sound comes out. There are many tape or video cassette lessons available from schools, libraries and stores which will help you with your pronunciation. You can also learn a lot by listening to the radio and watching television and films.

Pronunciation is often very difficult for native Asian-language speakers, because there are more sounds in English. In particular, there are a few more vowels in English than Indian. English speakers can easily tell the difference between "ham, him, hem" or "feet, fit, fed" for example.

The following series of pronunciation exercises combines words beginning with the same consonant sound followed by similar vowel sounds. Voiced and voiceless consonants are paired (b—voiced/p—voiceless, d—voiced / t—voiceless, etc.) to help students compare and contrast similar consonant formation.

U Sounding Vowels

'long uh' as in 'put'	*'short uh' as in 'up'*	*'oo' as in 'shoe'*
butcher	but	boot
put	pup	poof!
(none)	duck	do
Tokay	tough	tooth
good	gulp	Google
cook	cup	cool
soot	supper	suit
(none)	(none)	zoom
shook	shut	shoot
(none)	jump	June
churn	Chuck	choose
hook	hup!	who

Long Vowels and Consonants

'long ah' as in 'heart'	*'short ah' as in 'got'*
bar	bought
par	paw
dark	dot
tar	taught
Garth	got
carpet	caught
sergeant	saw
Zagreb	Zola
sharp	shawl
John	jot
charred	chocolate
heart	hop

Repeat each line slowly, listen for the minor differences between the vowel and consonant sounds. Repeat each line three times. Each time repeat more quickly trying to keep the sounds distinct. Find a partner and listen to each other repeat the lines. Try to invent sentences using each sound at least once. For example: The butcher put on his boots but he forgot his hat. Don't worry too much about the sentence making much sense!

Pronunciation of Dipthongs

A diphthong is a contour vowel—that is, a unitary vowel that changes quality during its pronunciation, or "glides", with a smooth movement of the tongue from one articulation to another, as in the English words eye, boy, and cow. This contrasts with "pure" vowels, or monophthongs, where the tongue is held still, as in the English word papa.

Diphthongs often form when separate vowels are run together in rapid speech during a conversation. However, there are also unitary diphthongs, as in the English examples above, which are heard by listeners as single-vowel sounds (phonemes).

When two vowel sounds blend together in a word, it is called a dipthong. Sometimes the sound is spelled with two letters and other times one letter does the job.

In fact, many of the Long Vowel sounds in English are called Dipthongs by language experts — A is really a blending of the A and E sounds, I is really a blending of the Soft A and E sounds, etc. To make matters more simple, however, in these lessons, we will treat the Long Vowel sounds as pure sounds. That leaves us with a few very definite Blended Vowel sounds, or Dipthongs.

Consonants are letters that are pronounced by forcing air through, over or between the various parts of your mouth: palate, teeth, tongue, lips. Sometimes the sound is made by stopping the flow of air and then releasing it. Again, examples of the correct pronunciation of these letters can be found elsewhere.

The following series of pronunciation exercises combines words beginning with the same diphthong sound followed by similar diphthong sounds. Voiced and voiceless consonants are paired (b - voiced / p - voiceless, d - voiced / t - voiceless, etc.) to help students compare and contrast similar consonant formation.

'ieh(r)' as in 'near'	*'ehi(r)' as in 'hair'*
beer	bear
peer	pear
dear	dare
tear (drop of water)	tear (rip)
gear	garish
clear	Claire
seer	snare
sheer	share
jeer	Jerry
cheer	chair
here	hair

These diphthongs are pronounced differently in British and American English. British English drops the 'r' sound and pronounces a slight 'uh' - 'hair' becomes 'hehuh'. In American English the 'r' is strongly pronounced - 'hair' becomes 'hehrrr'.

Pronounciating '-ed'

The past simple tense and past participle of all regular verbs end in -ed. For example:

base verb (v1)	*past simple (v2)*	*past participle (v3)*
work	worked	worked

In addition, many adjectives are made from the past participle and so end in -ed. For example:

– I like painted furniture.

The question is: How do we pronounce the -ed?

The answer is: In 3 ways - / Id/ or / t/ or / d/

If the base verb ends in one of these sounds		*example base verb*	*example with -ed:*	*pronounce the -ed:*	*extra syllable?*
unvoiced	/t/	want	wanted	/ Id/	yes
voiced	/d/	end	ended		
unvoiced	/p/	hope	hoped	/ t/	no
	/f/	laugh	laughed		
	/s/	fax	faxed		
	/S/	wash	washed		
	/tS/	watch	watched		
	/k/	like	liked		
voiced	all other sounds, for example...	play	played	/ d/	
		allow	allowed		
		beg	begged		

The following -ed words used as adjectives are pronounced with /Id/:

— aged	— dogged	— ragged
— blessed	— learned	— wicked
— crooked	— naked	— wretched

PRONOUNCIATING "THE"

Normally, we pronounce "the" with a short sound (like "thuh"). But when "the" comes before a vowel sound, we pronounce it as a long "thee".

vowel sound	*we write*	*we say*
A	the apple	thee apple
E	the egg	thee egg
I	the ice-cream	thee ice-cream
O	the orange	thee orange
U	the ugli fruit	thee ugli fruit

It is important to understand that it is what we say that matters, not what we write. It is the sound that matters, not the letter used in writing a word. So we use a long "thee" before a vowel sound, not necessarily before a vowel. Look at these cases:

we write	*with*	*we say*	*with*
the house	consonant (h)	thuh house	consonant sound
the hour	consonant (h)	thee our	vowel sound
the university	vowel (u)	thuh youniversity	consonant sound
the umbrella	vowel (u)	thee umbrella	vowel sound

When we wish to place emphasis on a particular word, we can use "emphatic the" [thee], whether or not the word begins with a consonant or vowel sound. For example:

— A: I saw the [thuh] President yesterday.

— B: What! The [thee] President of the United States?

— A: Yes, exactly.

PRONOUNCIATING 's'

If a word ends in the letter 's' (e.g. plural noun or verb in the third person), there are three ways to pronounce this 's' - /S/, /Z/ and /IZ/. Similarly, any word which ends in 'ed' (e.g. adjective or the past of a regular verb) may be pronounced either /T/, /D/ or /ID/.

Type One Sound /S/

In type one words, the final 's' should be pronounced with air pushed out between the top of your tongue and your top teeth, without using the vocal chords (the sound made by a snake or gas escaping from a pipe).

Type one sounds are used if the word ends in the following sounds:

Phonetic symbols	Example word
/p/	stops, ships
/t/	hits, pets
/k/	attacks, bricks
/f/	laughs, coughs
/θ/	maths, moths

These sounds are all unvoiced, which means that your vocal chords must be silent when you make the sound.

Type Two Sound /Z/

This sound is formed in the same way as type 1, but you must make a sound with your vocal chords (the sound made by a bee, or high-voltage electricity).

Type two sounds come after the following sounds:

Phonetic symbols	Example word
/b/	grabs, robs
/d/	lids, rods
/g/	pigs, dogs
/v/	loves, leaves
/D/	breathes, lathes
/l/	hills, fails
/m/	comes, trams
/n/	earns, burns
/N/	songs, paintings
any vowel sound	plays, employees, flees, goes, news

These sounds are all voiced, which means that your vocal chords must make a sound when you pronounce them.

Type Three Sound /IZ/

This sound is the same as the verb 'to be' in its third person form (is). Type three sounds are the only ones which add an additional syllable to the word, for example 'miss' /MIS/ is one syllable, but 'misses' /MIS IZ/ is two syllables. The final /IZ/ syllable isn't usually stressed.

Phonetic symbols	Example word
/s/	buses, places
/z/	chooses, sizes
/?/	washes, wishes
/t?/	watches, matches
/d? /	Judges, pages

10

Use of Slang

Slang is a type of language consisting of words and phrases that:

- are considered to be very informal
- are more common in speech than in writing
- are typically restricted to a particular group of people or context.

Slang is the use of informal words and expressions that are not considered standard in the speaker's dialect or language. Slang is often to be found in areas of the lexicon that refer to things considered taboo. It is also used to identify with one's peers.

Slang should be distinguished from jargon, which is the technical vocabulary of a particular profession. Jargon, like many examples of slang, may be used to exclude non–group members from the conversation, but in general has the function of allowing its users to talk precisely about technical issues in a given field.

Slang can be regional in that it is used only in a particular territory, but slang terms often are particular to a certain subculture, such as music. Nevertheless, slang expressions can spread outside their original areas to become commonly used, like "cool" and "jive." While some words eventually lose their status as slang (the word "mob", for example, began as a slang shortening of Latin mobile vulgus), others continue to be considered as such by most speakers. When slang spreads beyond the group or subculture that originally uses it, its original users often replace it with other, less-recognised terms to maintain group identity. One use of slang is to circumvent social taboos, as mainstream language tends to shy away from evoking certain realities. For this reason, slang vocabularies are particularly rich in certain domains, such as violence, crime, drugs, and sex. Alternatively, slang can grow out of mere familiarity with the things described. Among Californian wine connoisseurs, for example, Cabernet Sauvignon is often known as "Cab Sav," Chardonnay as "Chard" and so on; this means that naming the different wines expends less superfluous effort.

Even within a single language community, slang tends to vary widely across social, ethnic, economic, and geographic strata. Slang may fall into disuse over time; sometimes, however, it grows more and more common until it becomes the dominant way of saying something, at which time it usually comes to be regarded as mainstream, acceptable language (e.g. the Spanish word caballo), although in the case of taboo words there may be no expression that is considered mainstream or acceptable. Numerous slang terms pass into informal mainstream speech, and sometimes into formal speech, though this may involve a change in meaning or usage.

Slang very often involves the creation of novel meanings for existing words. It is common for such novel meanings to diverge significantly from the standard meaning. Thus, "cool" and "hot" can both mean "very good," "impressive," or "good-looking".

Slang may be all things to all people. According to the American poet Carl Sandburg (1878-1967), slang is "language which takes off its coat, spits on its hands—

and goes to work." The Concise Oxford Dictionary is more prosaic: "words, phrases, and uses that are regarded as very informal and are often restricted to special contexts or are peculiar to a specified profession, class, etc (racing slang; schoolboy slang)."

The problem for learners of English is to know when or when not to use slang. Many people condemn slang, but in fact we all use it. The trick is to use slang in the right context. For the learner, perhaps the first thing to remember is that slang is normally spoken, not written. The second thing is that you may wish to learn slang so that you can understand it when you hear it, but not necessarily to use it.

Slang words and expressions have crept into our everyday language, and so insiduously, that they have not been detected by the great majority of speakers, and so have become part and parcel of their vocabulary on an equal footing with the legitimate words of speech. They are called upon to do similar service as the ordinary words used in everyday conversation–to express thoughts and desires and convey meaning from one to another. In fact, in some cases, slang has become so useful that it has far outstripped classic speech and made for itself such a position in the vernacular that it would be very hard in some cases to get along without it. Slang words have usurped the place of regular words of language in very many instances and reign supreme in their own strength and influence.

Cant and slang are often confused in the popular mind, yet they are not synonymous, though very closely allied, and proceeding from a common Gypsy origin. Cant is the language of a certain class–the peculiar phraseology or dialect of a certain craft, trade or profession, and is not readily understood save by the initiated of such craft, trade or profession. It may be correct, according to the rules of grammar, but it is not universal; it is confined to certain parts and localities and is only intelligible to those for whom it is intended. In short, it is an esoteric language which only the initiated can understand. The jargon, or patter, of thieves is cant and it is only understood by thieves who have been let into its significance; the initiated language of professional gamblers is cant, and is only intelligible to gamblers.

On the other hand, slang, as it is nowadays, belongs to no particular class but is scattered all over and gets *entre* into every kind of society and is understood by all where it passes current in everyday expression. Of course, the nature of the slang, to a great extent, depends upon the locality, as it chiefly is concerned with colloquialisms or words and phrases common to a particular section. For instance, the slang of London is slightly different from that of New York, and some words in the one city may be unintelligible in the other, though well understood in that in which they are current. Nevertheless, slang may be said to be universally understood. "To kick the bucket," "to cross the Jordan," "to hop the twig" are just as expressive of the departing from life in the backwoods of America or the wilds of Australia as they are in London or Dublin.

Slang simply consists of words and phrases which pass current but are not refined, nor elegant enough, to be admitted into polite speech or literature whenever they are recognised as such. But, as has been said, a great many use slang without their knowing it as slang and incorporate it into their everyday speech and conversation. Some authors purposely use slang to give emphasis and spice in familiar and humorous writing, but they should not be imitated by the tyro. A master, such as Dickens, is forgivable, but in the novice it is unpardonable.

There are several kinds of slang attached to different professions and classes of society. For instance, there is college slang, political slang, sporting slang, etc. It is the nature of slang to circulate freely among all classes, yet there are several kinds of this current form of language corresponding to the several classes of society. The two great divisions of slang are the vulgar of the uneducated and coarse-minded, and the high-toned slang of the so-called upper classes–the educated and the wealthy. The hoyden of the gutter does not use the same slang as my lady in her boudoir, but both use it, and so expressive is it that the one might readily understand the other if brought in contact. Therefore, there are what may be styled an ignorant slang and an educated slang–the one common to the purlieus and the alleys, the other to the parlour and the drawing-room.

In all cases the object of slang is to express an idea in a more vigorous, piquant and terse manner than standard usage ordinarily admits. A school girl, when she wants to praise a baby, exclaims: "Oh, isn't he awfully cute!" To say that he is very nice would be too weak a way to express her admiration. When a handsome girl appears on the street an enthusiastic masculine admirer, to express his appreciation of her beauty, tells you: "She is a peach, a bird, a cuckoo," any of which accentuates his estimation of the young lady and is much more emphatic than saying: "She is a beautiful girl," "a handsome maiden," or "lovely young woman." When a politician defeats his rival he will tell you "it was a cinch," he had a "walk-over," to impress you how easy it was to gain the victory.

Some slang expressions are of the nature of metaphors and are highly figurative. Such are "to pass in your checks," "to hold up," "to pull the wool over your eyes," "to talk through your hat," "to fire out," "to go back on," "to make yourself solid with," "to have a jag on," "to be loaded," "to freeze on to," "to bark up the wrong tree," "don't monkey with the buzz-saw," and "in the soup." Most slang had a bad origin. The greater part originated in the cant of thieves' Latin, but it broke away from this cant of malefactors in time and gradually evolved itself from its unsavoury past until it developed into a current form of expressive speech. Some slang, however, can trace its origin back to very respectable sources.

America has had a large share in contributing to modern slang. "The heathen Chinee," and "Ways that are dark, and tricks that are vain," are from Bret Harte's *Truthful James*. "Not for Joe," arose during the Civil War when one soldier refused to give a drink to another. "Not if I know myself" had its origin in Chicago. "What's the matter with—? He's all right," had its beginning in Chicago also and first was "What's the matter with Hannah." referring to a lazy domestic servant. "There's millions in it," and "By a large majority" come from Mark Twain's *Gilded Age*. "Pull down your vest," "jim-jams," "got 'em bad," "that's what's the matter," "go hire a hall," "take in your sign," "dry up," "hump yourself," "it's the man around the corner," "putting up a job," "put a head on him," "no back talk," "bottom dollar," "went off on his ear," "chalk it down," "staving him off," "making it warm," "dropping him gently," "dead gone," "busted," "counter jumper," "put up or shut up," "bang up," "smart Aleck," "too much jaw," "chin-music," "top heavy," "barefooted on the top of the head," "a little too fresh," "champion liar," "chief cook and bottle washer," "bag and baggage," "as fine as silk," "name your poison," "died with his boots on," "old hoss," "hunkey dorey," "hold your horses," "galoot" and many others in use at present are all Americanisms in slang.

The newspapers are responsible for a large part of the slang. Reporters, staff writers, and even editors, put words and phrases into the mouths of individuals which they never utter. New York is supposed to be the headquarters of slang, particularly that portion of it known as the Bowery. All transgressions and corruptions of language are supposed to originate in that unclassic section, while the truth is that the laws of polite English are as much violated on Fifth Avenue. Of course, the foreign element mincing their "pidgin" English have given the Bowery an unenviable reputation, but there are just as good speakers of the vernacular on the Bowery as elsewhere in the greater city. Yet every inexperienced newspaper reporter thinks that it is incumbent on him to hold the Bowery up to ridicule and laughter, so he sits down, and out of his circumscribed brain, mutilates the English tongue (he can rarely coin a word), and blames the mutilation on the Bowery.

Current events, happenings of everyday life, often give rise to slang words, and these, after a time, come into such general use that they take their places in everyday speech like ordinary words and, as has been said, their users forget that they once were slang. For instance, the days of the Land League in Ireland originated the word *boycott*, which was the name of a very unpopular landlord, Captain Boycott. The people refused to work for him, and his crops rotted on the ground. From this time any one who came into disfavour and whom his neighbours refused to assist in any way was said to be boycotted. Therefore to boycott means to punish by abandoning or depriving a person of the assistance of others. At first it was a notoriously slang word, but now it is standard in the English dictionaries.

Politics add to our slang words and phrases. From this source we get "dark horse," "the gray mare is the better horse," "barrel of money," "buncombe," "gerrymander," "scalawag," "henchman," "logrolling," "pulling the wires," "taking the stump," "machine," "slate," etc. The money market furnishes us with "corner," "bull," "bear," "lamb," "slump," and several others.

The custom of the times and the requirements of current expression require the best of us to use slang words and phrases on occasions. Often we do not know they are slang, just as a child often uses profane words without consciousness of their being so. We should avoid the use of slang as much as possible, even when it serves to convey our ideas in a forceful manner. And when it has not gained a firm foothold in current speech it should be used not at all. Remember that most all slang is of vulgar origin and bears upon its face the bend sinister of vulgarity. Of the slang that is of good birth, pass it by if you can, for it is like a broken-down gentleman, of little good to any one. Imitate the great masters as much as you will in classical literature, but when it comes to their slang, draw the line.

Other Books on

WORD POWER SERIES

1. School Essays, Letters, Applications, and Stories For Higher Secondary Students **(New)**
2. Idiomatic English **(New)**
3. Effective English Comprehension Read Fast, Understand Better ! **(New)**
4. Latest Essays for College & Competitive Examinations **(New)**
5. Dictionary of New Words **(New)**
6. Art of English Conversation Speak English Fluently **(New)**
7. Teach Yourself English Grammar & Composition
8. Common & Uncommon Proverbs **(New)**
9. Effective Editing Help Yourself in Becoming a Good Editor **(New)**
10. Effective English A Boon for Learners **(New)**
11. Essays for Primary Classes
12. Essays for Junior Classes
13. Essays for Senior Classes
14. Dictionary of Synonyms and Antonyms
15. Dictionary of Idioms and Phrases
16. Common Phrases
17. How to Write & Speak Correct English
18. Meaningful Quotes
19. Punctuation Book
20. Top School Essays
21. How to Write Business Letters with CD
22. Everyday Grammar
23. Everyday Conversation
24. Letters for All Occasions

25. School Essays & Letters for Juniors
26. Common Mistakes in English
27. The Power of Writing
28. Learn English in 21 Lessons
29. First English Dictionary
30. Boost Your Spelling Power
31. Self-Help to English Conversation
32. The Art of Effective Communication
33. A Book of Proverbs & Quotations
34. Word Power Made Easy
35. English Grammar Easier Way
36. General English for Competitive Examinations
37. Spoken English
38. School Essays, Letters Writing and Phrases
39. How to Write & Speak Better English
40. Quote Unquote (A Handbook of Famous Quotations)
41. Improve Your Vocabulary
42. Common Errors in English
43. The Art of Effective Letter Writing
44. Synonyms & Antonyms
45. Idioms
46. Business Letters

Unit No. 220, Second Floor, 4735/22,
Prakash Deep Building, Ansari Road, Darya Ganj,
New Delhi - 110002, Ph. : 41325510, 9811838000
E-mail: lotuspress1984@gmail.com, www.lotuspress.co.in